THE VANDERBILT CAMPUS

A Pictorial History

Robert A. McGaw

THE
VANDERBILT CAMPUS

A Pictorial History

ROBERT A. McGAW

VANDERBILT UNIVERSITY PRESS ❧ NASHVILLE

Second printing, April 1979.

Library of Congress Cataloging in Publication Data

McGaw, Robert A., 1914—
  The Vanderbilt campus.

  Includes index.
  1. Vanderbilt University, Nashville—Pictorial works — History.
I. Vanderbilt University, Nashville. II. Title.
LD5588.M33   378.768'55   78-9913
ISBN 0-8265-1210-0

Printed in the United States of America

Contents

Acknowledgments

This book had its beginning in an exhibit mounted in the corridors of Kirkland Hall April 28, 1974, the day Vanderbilt celebrated the centennial of the campus by observing the hundredth anniversary of the laying of the cornerstone of that first building. The exhibit owed its visual appeal to the artistry of Robert A. Baldwin, who designed it, and of J. Clark Thomas, who made most of the newer photographs and copied older ones from the archives. The exhibit is expanded and updated by the book, which contains considerably more text and almost twice as many pictures.

The book would hardly have been possible without the Vanderbilt Photographic Archive, which in four years since its modest start in 1974 gathered many pictures from scattered places and made them secure as well as accessible. I am therefore especially indebted to Kay Russell Beasley and her predecessors in the office, J. Clark Thomas and Beth Tanner.

Grateful am I for having known personally a good many close observers of the Vanderbilt scene. Two who did the most over the longest time to save the pictorial record of the University's history were John T. McGill and Stella Vaughn. Dr. McGill entered Vanderbilt as a student in 1876 and scarcely left the place until he died in 1946, professor emeritus, age 94. Miss Stella came at age ten in 1882, when her father joined the faculty, and lived on the campus or a block away until she died in 1960. Aileen Bishop was another savior of Vanderbilt ephemera while serving from 1915 to 1958 as secretary to Chancellors Kirkland, Carmichael, and Branscomb. Edward Bryan knew every cranny of the campus and saw that the records of the physical plant were kept in good order from the time he was given responsibility for it in 1924 until he retired in 1971.

Thanks to them and other individuals working on their own, partly from sense of duty but more from love of subject, reminders of Vanderbilt's past were saved for it during the first ninety years. Not until 1963 did the University institutionalize its archives by policy, a budget, and appointment of persons trained for the task. Custody of the archival materials was assigned to the Special Collections of the Joint University Libraries, where Marice Wolfe has had responsibility since 1973.

For the basic facts of campus development, my main reliance was on complete sets of the University's annual catalogs and minutes of the Board of Trust. Many other sources were consulted to fill out the narrative and to illustrate it. Only one formal book-length history of the University has been published, that by Edwin Mims in 1946. It was preceded by his biography of Chancellor Kirkland in 1940 and followed in 1955 by John J. Tigert's biography of Bishop Holland Nimmons McTyeire. An illustrated story of the Engineering School's first century, *10² Years*, was published by Dillard Jacobs in 1975. A specialized study of Landon Garland is being prepared for publication by Robert T. Lagemann. The most useful periodicals were the *Vanderbilt University Quarterly*, which was published from 1901 to 1915, and the *Vanderbilt Alumnus* since then. The students began publishing their year-book in 1887, calling it *The Comet*, a name changed to *The Commodore* in 1909. Several of the pictures in this book are from them.

To all the photographers, draftsmen, and painters who are represented herein, I express my appreciation and my gratitude.

Finally, I thank Chancellors Harvie Branscomb and Alexander Heard and President Emmett Fields for affording me the privilege of being on this campus and for the opportunity to tell about it.

Robert A. McGaw

Donald Davidson, who died in 1968, was long Vanderbilt's man of letters—poet, essayist, historian, teacher of writing. For years his poem beginning "Morning was golden" was printed in the *V-Book* given to entering freshmen, and it was set to music by Cyrus Daniel in 1973 for the Centennial of the University's founding. When Professor Davidson was asked in 1963 how the poem came about, he wrote this answer beneath the verses:

My recollection is that these verses were written not long after the Vanderbilt Semi-Centennial Celebration of 1925. The University employed a professional advertising firm to work up promotional material for the Four Million Dollar Campaign. Somehow or other, I was called into the office of one of these professionals—in the then new Alumni Building. I believe. This man showed me the layout of a brochure and asked me if I could write some verses to fit under the photographs of buildings—photographs taken not only to show off the buildings, but students passing back and forth among the buildings, in and out the doors. There was a fine play of light and movement in these handsome photographs. I agreed to try to fill the required spaces with suitable verses. The difficulty was that the spaces were not uniform. Furthermore, the photographs did not come one after another, in a group, but were scattered. Each space filling group of verses must be a unit in itself, to fit a picture. But how could I give the poem as a whole any unity? After a considerable struggle, I finally came up with the above poem, which was accepted and printed—in a distributed form—in the brochure. It should be remembered that only Alumni and Neely (and the Medical School building) were new then. The old predominated! The paths, the trees, the grass were as they had been for half a century.

Morning was golden when from one high tower

The cool bell stirred its bronze and rang the hour.

Trees were all April to our youthful mood,

And sun lit golden Morning in the blood;

For what is Morning but to tread old ways

Where other steps have trod, and measure days

With eager touch as for an ancient door

That willingly swings as it has swung before?

Where youthful feet have passed and yet will pass

Morning abides on trees and tower and grass;

And Morning rules where voices murmuring

From April windows summon up the Spring.

Old paths may change, new faces light old walls,

Morning will still be golden in these halls.

Donald Davidson, '17

The first four lines
of Donald Davidson's poem
were first published
under this photograph
in 1926.

MAP OF THE
**Battlefield of
Nashville.**
Dec. 15-16th, 1864.
Drawn by Wilbur F. Foster,
Major Engineer Corps, C. S. A.

Rand, McNally & Co., Eng'rs, Chicago.

This rusted iron tethering stake was unearthed in 1951 during the excavation for Frederick Vanderbilt Hall. The supposition is that a Union cavalryman lost it there during the battle of Nashville.

On Wilbur Foster's map of the battlefield, the lines of the city's fortifications run from river to river. Land that became the Vanderbilt campus a decade later is where the last word, Forces, ends the legend, Interior Line Manned by Quarter-Master Forces.

The Situation

In February 1862, early in the Civil War, Nashville was occupied by the Union army, and the city that had been a center of supplies, transport, and communication for the Confederate forces became a larger one for the Union. To defend it against recapture, the occupation authorities saw to the erection of a line of forts and breastworks that made Nashville the most strongly fortified city in America by the time the Confederates tried desperately, in December 1864, to retake it. The inner line of defense crossed what would become, in the next decade, the Vanderbilt campus.

Two miles south of that point, the Confederate army formed its main line after coming on toward Nashville from Franklin, where it had lost more than 6,000 men in the bloody battle there. The Union army moved out of its fortified positions and attacked. The result was a rout of the Confederates, complete victory for the Union, and the inevitable end of the war four months later.

The war had interrupted efforts, begun in the 1850s, to establish in Nashville a university under the auspices of the Methodist Episcopal Church, South. Efforts revived after the war, and a charter was obtained August 6, 1872.

The situation was described later by Bishop Holland N. McTyeire, the chief organizer of the project, in these words:

"Such, however, was the exhausted condition of the South, and so slow its recuperation under the disorganized state of its labor, trade, and governments, that the first efforts to raise funds showed the impossibility of the enterprise . . . and the well-laid scheme was already—in the judgment of some of its warmest friends—a failure."

At that crisis, according to the Bishop's account of events, Cornelius Vanderbilt "stepped forward and, by his princely gift, gave form and substance to the plan."

The Commodore's initial donation was $500,000, which he afterward increased to a million dollars for

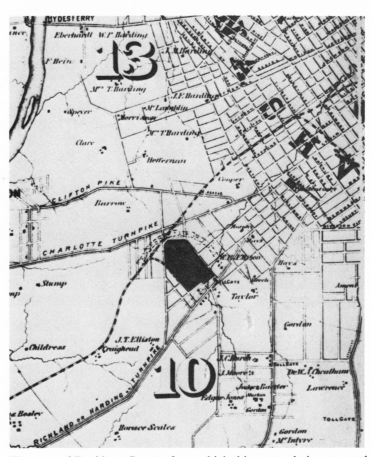

The map of Davidson County from which this rectangle is extracted was also drawn by Wilbur F. Foster. The year was 1871. Land that became the Vanderbilt campus lies across Harding Turnpike from the Tennessee Fair Grounds (now Centennial Park) and is identified further by the names BEECH and TAYLOR, who were the owners and residents of the only two houses that were on the property.

building and endowing the university that had existed only on paper.

Sectional sentiment was still strong. "A citizen of the North," McTyeire wrote, "Mr. Vanderbilt could have found there ready acceptance of his gift, and built up an

Frank Crawford Vanderbilt, the Commodore's second wife, was from Mobile, Alabama, and was a cousin of Bishop McTyeire's wife. She was influential in her husband's decision to found a university in the South.

In his *History of Vanderbilt University,* Edwin Mims wrote: "It is said on good authority that when the Bishop and the Commodore were discussing the plans, the Commodore, on looking over a railroad map, observed that Nashville was a strategic center, easy of access, for the whole region. When he was told that the Church had put the Publishing House there and that its connectional offices were all centered there, the question of location was settled."

institution rivaling those which abound in that wealthier and more prosperous section of the country; but to the South he looked, and extended to her people what they needed as much as pecuniary aid—*a token of good-will.* The act, timely and delicately as munificently done, touched men's hearts. It had no conditions that wounded the self-respect, or questioned the patriotism, of the recipients. The effect was widely healing and reconciling, as against any sectional animosities which the late unhappy years had tended to create."

The Commodore made his gift subject to five conditions, of which the first three stipulated the confidence that he placed in Bishop McTyeire. The fourth stated that the endowment portion of his gift "shall be forever inviolable, and shall be kept safely invested, and the interest or revenue, only, used in carrying on the University." The fifth and last said, "The University is to be located in or near Nashville, Tennessee."

From *Frank Leslie's Illustrated Newspaper,* April 17, 1875.

The Founding

Commodore Cornelius Vanderbilt of New York gave a million dollars to build and endow this university at a time when the South was impoverished by the Civil War. March 17, 1873, was the date of his founding gift. On April 28, 1874, the cornerstone was laid. After the university opened for classes in October 1875, he wrote to Bishop McTyeire:

"I tender my personal expressions of extreme regard, trusting that the healthful growth of the institution may be as great as I know it is your desire and determination to make it—and if it shall, through its influence, contribute, even in the smallest degree, to strengthening the ties which should exist between all geographical sections of our common country, I shall feel that it has accomplished one of the objects that led me to take an interest in it."

That was his only recorded statement of purpose. Cornelius Vanderbilt died in 1877 at age 82 without ever seeing the university that bears his name.

In 1875 artist Jared Flagg put a sketch of the Main Building under the Commodore's silk hat in this portrait. At right, enlarged.

13

Bishop Holland McTyeire led a movement within the Methodist Episcopal Church, South, to establish a university, but efforts failed for lack of money in the region. Mrs. McTyeire and Mrs. Vanderbilt, both from Mobile, were cousins. The Bishop visited the Vanderbilts in New York and won the Commodore's admiration and support.

The Commodore entrusted the Bishop with authority to procure suitable grounds, erect suitable buildings, and administer the institution. Some land was obtained by purchase, some by gift. In a letter to the Commodore, McTyeire described the site as "west of the city, beautiful for situation, easy of approach, and of the same elevation as Capitol Hill, which is in full view." The McTyeires moved into the house known now as Old Central where he could supervise the planning and construction of the new university. The Bishop himself planted young trees all over the place. And he, along with Chancellor Garland, assembled the first faculty.

McTyeire was President of the Board of Trust, which at that time meant chief executive of the University, until he died in 1889.

Holland McTyeire at age 42, soon after his election as Bishop in 1866. He moved to Nashville a year later.

Oldest.

This bur oak tree
(Quercus macrocarpa) is the
oldest living thing on
campus, perhaps 300 years,
and Old Central is the
oldest building, erected
about 1859 as a residence
by Mr. and Mrs. Henry Foote.
Its land was hers by
inheritance. He had been
Governor of Mississippi, and
during the Civil War he
represented Tennessee in the
Confederate States Congress.
Bishop McTyeire lived in the
house from 1873 to 1875 while
overseeing construction of the
first Vanderbilt buildings.
Since then it has housed
faculty families, students,
the English Department, and,
since 1972, the Graduate Program
in Economic Development.

All the land in the original Vanderbilt campus of 75 acres was first owned by John Cockrill, gunsmith and brother-in-law of James Robertson, who founded Nashville in what was then western North Carolina during the American Revolution. Robertson led the pioneers who walked 450 miles from their starting point on the Holston River. Cockrill arrived in April 1780 with the main body of settlers—men, women, and children—who floated flatboats down the Holston and Tennessee rivers in midwinter and pulled and poled them up the Ohio and Cumberland at spring flood, a daring voyage of 1,000 miles.

Among those who came by boat was the widow Ann Robertson Johnston, who married John Cockrill in the

This leaning tree, an overcup oak, was mentioned in early deeds because it marked a corner common to three tracts of land— those labeled *B, C,* and *E* on the opposite page. The terrace of Rand Hall covers the spot now. The tree came to be called "The Garland Oak" because the first Chancellor's house was near and he placed boxes for squirrels in it. In this old view, the camera looked straight down Twenty-third Avenue. The foundation of Kissam Hall is visible on the left. The ancient tree fell about 1915.

fall of 1780 at Fort Nashborough, James Robertson presiding. Cockrill claimed 640 acres of land surrounding a big spring where Natchez Trace now enters West End Avenue. A granite boulder farther inside Centennial Park is about where they built a double log house in which they lived until 1814. A bronze plaque on the boulder is a tribute to Ann as Nashville's first schoolteacher.

In 1923 John T. McGill, Professor of Chemistry and tireless recorder of Vanderbilt history, traced the boundaries of Cockrill's square mile in relation to modern placenames. The two corners nearest the campus were the southeast, which McGill located about fifty feet east of Peabody's Psychology Building, and the northeast, near the intersection of Seventeenth Avenue, North, and State Street. He also traced the transactions that led finally, in 1873, to deeds in the hands of Bishop McTyeire, acting as trustee for Vanderbilt University. On the opposite page, heavy black lines and letters are superimposed on a recent map to outline parcels that McTyeire put together to make the original campus. Letters *A, B,* and *D* represent, in that order: land bought from C. A. R. Thompson, who had planned to build a home where Kirkland Hall is now; A. B. Beech, who was living in the house now called Old Central; and Daniel Dougheny, whose tract cornered at West End and Twenty-first. All three of these owners had bought their land from Mrs. Rachel Boyd Foote, whose grandfather, John Boyd, acquired it from John Cockrill, part in 1798, part in 1807. The largest tract, labeled *C,* was bought from Jane Litton Taylor, granddaughter of John Childress, who bought it from Cockrill in 1803. *E* is for Mrs. Elizabeth B. Elliston, whose father-in-law, Joseph T. Elliston, bought from the Cockrills in 1821, the year Ann died.

The site was McTyeire's choice after considering several alternatives, of which the last to be eliminated was across the Cumberland River in Edgefield. Total value of the acquisitions was $89,750, of which $15,250 was the value of portions donated by owners. Nashvillians contributed, in addition, about $28,000.

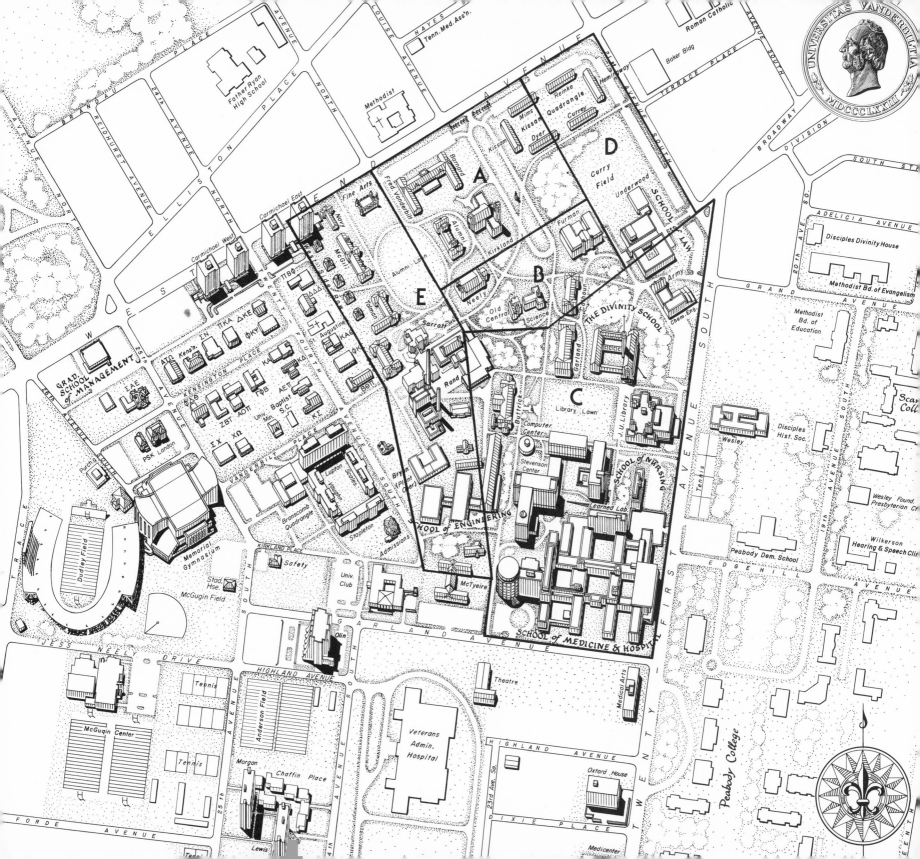

William C. Smith of Nashville was the architect of Vanderbilt's first buildings. They consisted of the Main Building (now Kirkland Hall), the astronomical observatory (razed in 1952 when Rand was built), and eight residences, of which two remain. There were also two older houses of which one, Old Central, yet stands. Classrooms, the library, laboratories, the chapel, offices all were in the Main Building. The campus of 75 acres was bounded, as now, by West End Avenue and what is now Twenty-first, but stopped at Garland Avenue and the alley that is behind West Side Row. The schools of Law and Medicine were housed elsewhere in Nashville. Population of the city then was 40,000. Vanderbilt's enrollment was 307.

Smith was later the architect for the replica of the Parthenon for the 1897 Tennessee Centennial Exposition.

Architect William C. Smith.

Cornerstone was laid April 28, 1874.

Opposite page: This, the earliest known photograph of Vanderbilt, shows the "Main Building" as it looked in 1875, when it opened for classes. Bishop McTyeire's two-horse carriage is at far right.

19

At left: Garland saw to the design and specifications of the Observatory. The telescope—a six-inch refractor made by Cooke & Sons in York, England—was used most successfully by young Edward Barnard to watch for comets. He discovered sixteen of them in all, in Nashville and later at Lick Observatory in California, where he discovered the fifth satellite of Jupiter.

Below: Named for Barnard, the Observatory eventually was made useless by smog and city lights. It was razed in 1952 to clear the site for Rand Hall. The telescope was remounted in 1972/73 on the roof of Stevenson Center for the Natural Sciences.

Landon C. Garland had taught the younger McTyeire at Randolph-Macon College in Virginia. He became the president of Randolph-Macon and in 1855 was named president of the University of Alabama. After the Civil War destroyed that university he taught eight years at the University of Mississippi. At age 65 he was elected Vanderbilt's first Chancellor. He served in that office from 1875 until 1893 and for two years longer as Professor of Physics and Astronomy.

He is buried on the campus next to Bishop McTyeire.

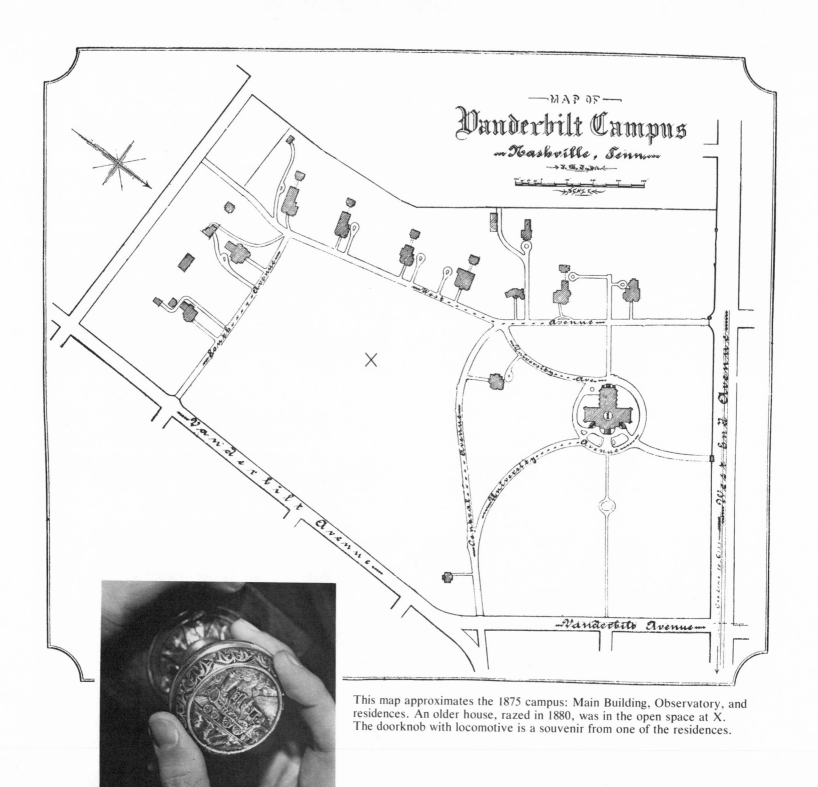

MAP OF

Vanderbilt Campus

Nashville, Tenn.

This map approximates the 1875 campus: Main Building, Observatory, and residences. An older house, razed in 1880, was in the open space at X. The doorknob with locomotive is a souvenir from one of the residences.

This was Bishop McTyeire's house from 1875 until he died in 1889. At the time of this photograph it was Chancellor Kirkland's. On the map opposite, it is the larger of the two houses at far left, facing northward. It stood where the Zerfoss Student Health Center was built in 1967.

Chancellor Garland's house was this one, which on the map is next southward from the Observatory. It was razed along with the Observatory in 1952 to provide a site for Rand Hall. Behind each residence was a two-room cottage for servants.

23

Homes for Faculty

When the University opened for classes in October 1875
there were nine residences on campus for faculty,
counting Old Central *(pictured on page 15)* and the homes
of Bishop McTyeire and Chancellor Garland *(page 23)*.
Next to Garland's was the one shown above in two views,
old and recent. When covered with vines it was the home
of William J. Vaughn, Professor of Mathematics and
Astronomy, who lived there from 1884 until 1912.
On the right it is labeled "Western Civilization," a sign
of its current use as offices for graduate fellows
of the Department of History.

This was not one of the original homes for faculty
but was built in 1900 and placed between
the Garland and Vaughn homes as a substitute for
one razed to clear the site for old Kissam Hall.
Pictured during the period, beginning in the 1940s,
when it was headquarters for the Student Christian
Association, it later housed Germanic Languages
and, most recently, the Afro-American Association.

Upper right: Another survivor is this house,
"Number 7," which stands next to McTyeire Hall and
in 1978 housed the Center for Health Services.

This house was razed in 1899 to clear the site for Kissam Hall.

Marble bust of Landon Garland is in the Stevenson Center for the Natural Sciences along with a display of antique equipment from the Garland Collection of Classical Physics Apparatus. The collection includes more than two hundred items, most of them purchased on a trip he made to Europe in the spring of 1875. As a result, when Vanderbilt opened that fall it was said to have scientific equipment equal to any university in America.

John Adamson '56 and James Patton '55, back on campus for Alumni Reunion, inspected the sundial they made when they were engineering students under the instruction of Professor Dillard Jacobs, who designed it. Since 1964 the armillary-type dial has been an attractive feature on the terrace of Rand Hall. A plaque records that the octagonal base "is built of bricks and stone salvaged from Barnard Observatory, which stood on this site from 1875 until it was razed in 1952. The University named the building for Edward Emerson Barnard in proud testimony that here, from 1883 to 1887, he prepared for his great career in astronomy."

Three Bishops and Garland

"Under the shade of magnolias that his own hand planted, he sleepeth well," said Chancellor Kirkland in his 1893 inaugural address when speaking of Bishop McTyeire, who was then only four years in his grave at the center of the campus. In 1876 McTyeire had seen to the reburial here of two other bishops, both of whom had died in the Nashville area much earlier and whose graves were neglected.

One was William McKendree, first American-born Methodist bishop, who had been a soldier with Washington when Cornwallis surrendered. The other was Joshua Soule, who, though Maine-born and descendant of Mayflower pilgrims, led in forming the Methodist Episcopal Church, South. When Chancellor Garland died in 1895, his body also was buried here. The same magnolias cast shade in 1978.

Main Building, *i.e.,* Kirkland Hall

It has been called Main Building, University Hall, College Hall, and now Kirkland Hall in honor of Vanderbilt's second Chancellor and his wife. The upper pictures on the opposite page show it, front and rear, as it looked when new. Perhaps the twin towers' roofs leaked; there are pictures showing first one, then both towers with flat roofs in place of the sloping originals. Calamity came April 20, 1905, when fire gutted the building and consumed much of its contents, including all but 4,900 of the 23,500 books in the main library.

The next day, classes met elsewhere—on schedule. William Kissam Vanderbilt, grandson of the Commodore, responded to the emergency with $150,000 for rebuilding. Alumni and Nashvillians gave about $50,000.

Rebuilt immediately, steel trusses were fitted into the thick brick walls, and reinforced concrete replaced the burned timber floors. The Victorian Gothic style of the original structure gave way to a more forceful Italianate. The town hall of Siena, a fourteenth century masterpiece, served as a model for the battlements around the roof and for the one tall belltower that became Vanderbilt's architectural symbol.

Town Hall of Siena, Italy.

Reconstruction after the fire of 1905. The outlines of an original wooden truss are scorched on bricks of the rear wall.

Main Building, 1875. *Below:* Later view, with altered towers.

Rear view, 1877. *Below:* After the fire of April 20, 1905.

Architects for rebuilding after the fire
were Carpenter & Blair, New York. J. Edwin
Carpenter was a Tennessean trained
at Massachusetts Institute of Technology
and Ecole des Beaux Arts in Paris.

Picture at left shows the terra cotta
gargoyle downspouts near top of tower.
Weakened by weather, they were removed
in 1960 and the balconies cut back
to avert the danger of breaking loose.

The tower rises 170 feet above ground.

This 1920s snapshot from the tower includes
gargoyle, Commodore's statue, and part
of the road that circled the building then.

The chapel on the third floor served
its original purpose fifty years until
Neely Auditorium was built. After 1925 it
was the reading room of the University's
main library, and after 1941 the Law School's.
In 1968 the space was converted to
three floors of offices.

After the fire of 1905, children gave coins
toward replacing the clock and buying
a new bronze bell of 2,000 pounds weight.
On the bell are cast words, "Gift of the children
to Vanderbilt University—1906—Ring in the
Nobler Mode of Life."

The weight-driven clock wore out and was
replaced by electric timers in 1966.
Aluminum hands, colored gold, replaced
the gilded wood originals, one of which
was this minute hand, four feet long.

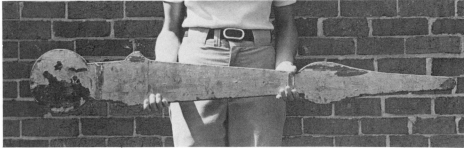

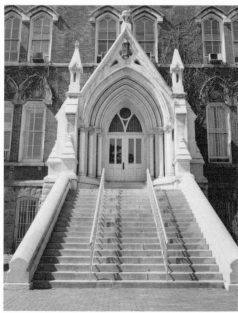

32

Left:
Kirkland Hall in 1974
and details of the doorway,
unchanged for a century.

Right:
A moot court in session, 1957.
The School of Law was housed
in the building from 1875
to 1889, when it moved downtown
to a building that is pictured
on page 68. It was housed again
in the main building from
January 1916 to September 1962.

The Commodore's Statue

Nashville citizens—mainly the officers of the Tennessee Centennial Exposition—subscribed to pay for the statue of Cornelius Vanderbilt. The sculptor was Giuseppe Moretti, native Italian whose studio was in New York, where the figure was modeled and cast. This photograph, the earliest known showing the statue in place on the campus, was made sometime between the years 1897 and 1905.

The statue's first location was at the west end of the Parthenon during the Tennessee Centennial Exposition in the summer of 1897. When the exposition closed that fall it was moved to the campus.

The statue has faced north since 1949, when the main entrance to the campus was placed on West End Avenue.

Inscribed on the granite pedestal is Cornelius Vanderbilt's only recorded statement of purpose in founding the University.

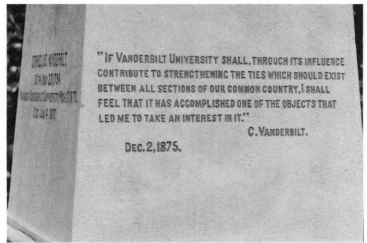

The Old Gym ❧ Victorian Gothic Preserved

The two photographs above
are reproduced from *The Comet*
of 1887, published by students.
It was the first volume in
the series of yearbooks that
became *The Commodore* in 1909.

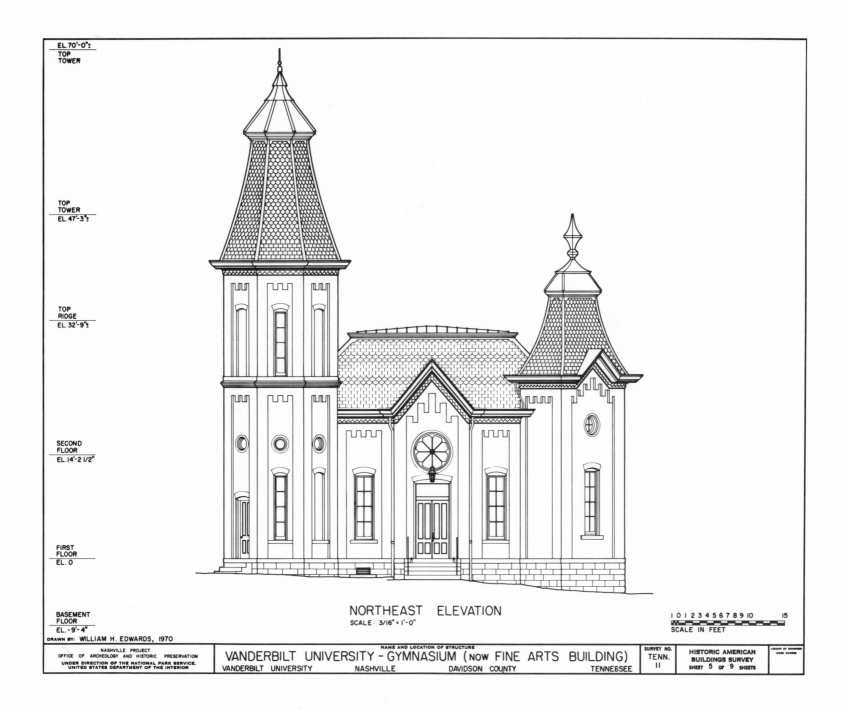

EL.70'-0":
TOP
TOWER

TOP
TOWER
EL. 47'-3"½

TOP
RIDGE
EL. 32'-9"½

SECOND
FLOOR
EL. 14'-2 1/2"

FIRST
FLOOR
EL. 0

BASEMENT
FLOOR
EL. -9'-4"

DRAWN BY: WILLIAM H. EDWARDS, 1970

NORTHEAST ELEVATION
SCALE: 3/16" = 1'-0"

1 0 1 2 3 4 5 6 7 8 9 10   15
SCALE IN FEET

NASHVILLE PROJECT
OFFICE OF ARCHEOLOGY AND HISTORIC PRESERVATION
UNDER DIRECTION OF THE NATIONAL PARK SERVICE.
UNITED STATES DEPARTMENT OF THE INTERIOR

NAME AND LOCATION OF STRUCTURE
VANDERBILT UNIVERSITY - GYMNASIUM (NOW FINE ARTS BUILDING)
VANDERBILT UNIVERSITY   NASHVILLE   DAVIDSON COUNTY   TENNESSEE

SURVEY NO.
TENN.
11

HISTORIC AMERICAN
BUILDINGS SURVEY
SHEET 5 OF 9 SHEETS

LIBRARY OF CONGRESS
INDEX NUMBER

Respect for the external charm of this Victorian Gothic gem, designed by Peter J. Williamson in 1880, controlled Vanderbilt's 1961 remodeling of the interior to accommodate the Department of Fine Arts. In 1970 the structure was recorded in exact graphic detail by a team of architectural draftsmen, followed by photographer Jack Boucher, all working for the Historic American Buildings Survey of the U. S. Department of the Interior. Subsequently the building was placed on the National Register of Historic Places. The original drawings and photographs are in the Library of Congress. Several are reproduced here on pages 36 through 40.

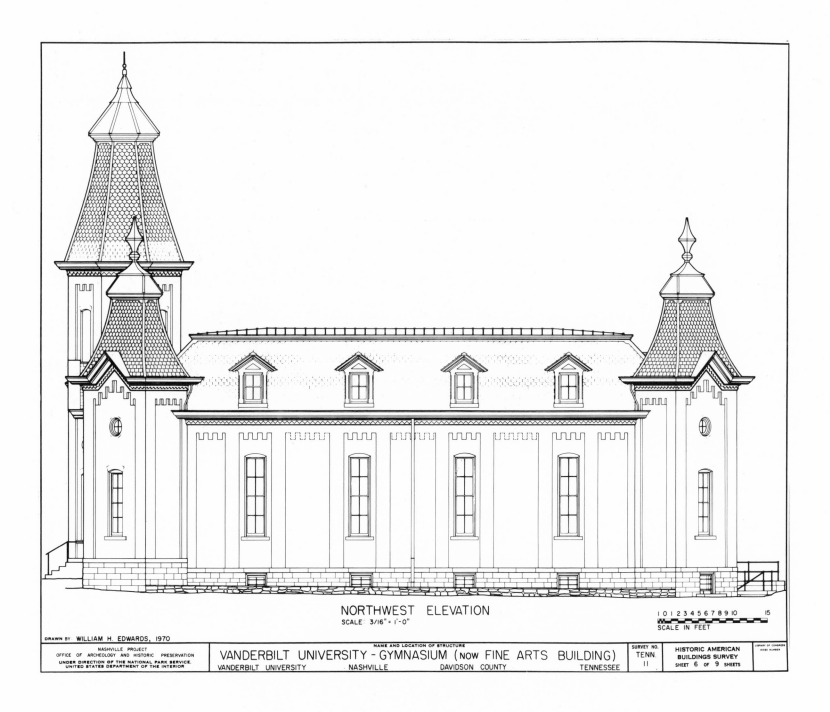

NORTHWEST ELEVATION
SCALE: 3/16" = 1'-0"

1 0 1 2 3 4 5 6 7 8 9 10   15
SCALE IN FEET

DRAWN BY WILLIAM H. EDWARDS, 1970

NASHVILLE PROJECT
OFFICE OF ARCHEOLOGY AND HISTORIC PRESERVATION
UNDER DIRECTION OF THE NATIONAL PARK SERVICE.
UNITED STATES DEPARTMENT OF THE INTERIOR.

NAME AND LOCATION OF STRUCTURE
VANDERBILT UNIVERSITY - GYMNASIUM (NOW FINE ARTS BUILDING)
VANDERBILT UNIVERSITY   NASHVILLE   DAVIDSON COUNTY   TENNESSEE

SURVEY NO.
TENN.
11

HISTORIC AMERICAN
BUILDINGS SURVEY
SHEET 6 OF 9 SHEETS

LIBRARY OF CONGRESS
INDEX NUMBER

39

Mr. and Mrs. William H. Vanderbilt and
painting of his great-great-grandfather,
the Commodore. Occasion was the exhibit,
"Portraits of Vanderbilts," during the
1973 celebration of the Centennial of
the Founding of the University.

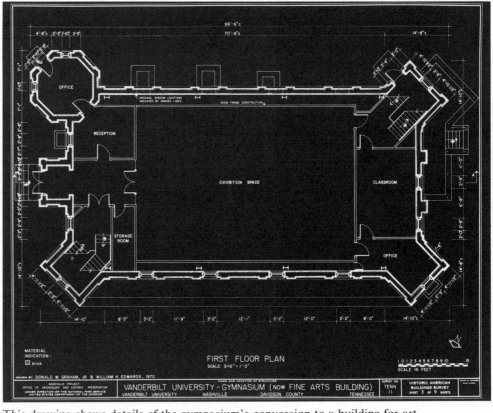

This drawing shows details of the gymnasium's conversion to a building for art.

Gymnasium Annex, added in 1920, was removed in 1964. It was 50 by 100 feet.
Basketball games were played in it in the '20s; the team practiced here until 1952.

At right:
Gym Dance, 1947/48.

1880s ❦ *'On the city's western border, Reared against the sky'*

The first words of Vanderbilt's *Alma Mater* truly describe the look of the campus in 1880 when the woodcut on the opposite page was made. All the buildings at that time were placed on or near the crest of the hill for their best view of the city and the city's best view of them. Placement of the buildings relative to each other was scarcely considered beyond the need that they be a brief walk apart.

The Victorian era was at its zenith, and architects expressed Victorian style exuberantly at Vanderbilt. Peter J. Williamson—who studied architecture in Holland before the Civil War, fought for the Union, and settled in Nashville afterward—designed the old Gymnasium, old Wesley *(left below),* and old Science *(right below)* all in 1880. Olin Landreth, Vanderbilt's first Professor of Engineering, was architect for West Side Row (1886) and West Side Hall (1887).

From 1880 until it burned in 1932, Wesley Hall housed the Divinity School. It faced Twenty-first and stood where Library Lawn is now.

Science Hall's location has thwarted planners because it is aligned with neither of the campus's main axes but stands where they meet.

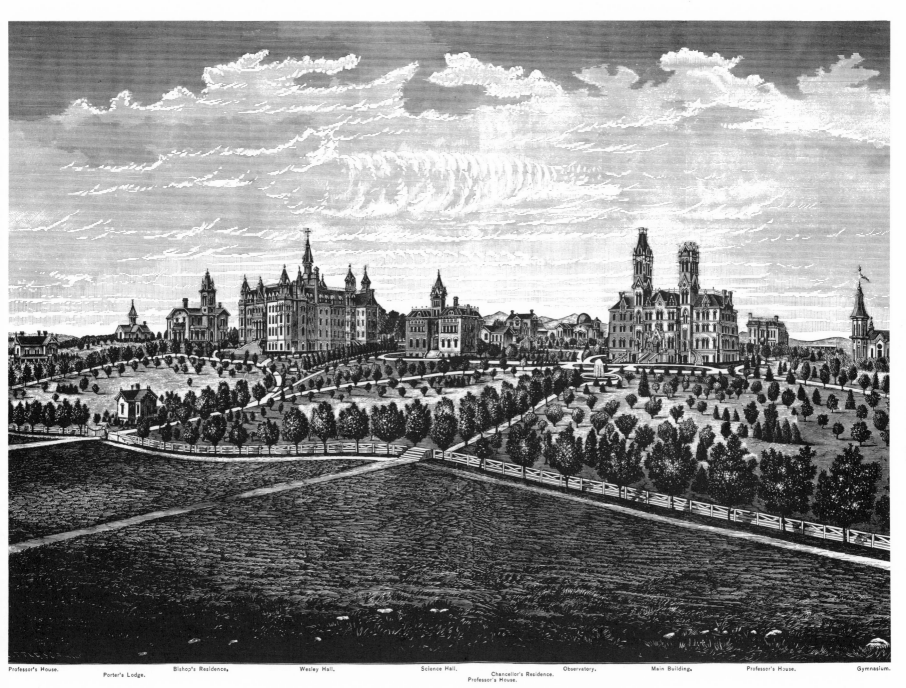

Professor's House.		Bishop's Residence.								Observatory.		Main Building.		Professor's House.		Gymnasium.
Porter's Lodge.			Wesley Hall.		Science Hall.		Chancellor's Residence.								
							Professor's House.								

(*Residences of four Professors out of view.*)

VANDERBILT UNIVERSITY, NASHVILLE, TENNESSEE.

Sketched by H. P. Whinnery.

43

Old Wesley Hall dominates the view of the campus from across Twenty-first Avenue in this picture, in which the steeple of old Science Hall and the tower of the Main Building also rise above the treetops. The photo was made about the time when old Wesley's main occupant, the Divinity School, was barely surviving the University's new independence. Official break with the Methodist Episcopal Church, South, came in 1915 as aftermath of a decision by the Tennessee Supreme Court that it is the Board of Trust's right to elect its own members. The Church abandoned its connection with Vanderbilt and established two other universities,
Emory in Atlanta and Southern Methodist in Dallas.

The cafeteria in Wesley opened in 1921 and was a popular place to eat, especially for townspeople on Sundays after attending church in the vicinity. (There had been a dining room, off and on, from the beginning, but it had been closed for years.)

The first Vanderbilt catalogue published the following statement:

"The University does not provide board and rooms for those in attendance. Students are allowed to select their own homes in families approved by the Faculty. There are no dormitories connected with the Institution, and none are contemplated, except as may hereafter be supplied in connection with the Divinity School. For the generality of young men, the dormitory system is unsatisfactory in its results. In the opinion of most persons best qualified to judge, it is injurious to both morals and manners. It is thought far safer to disperse young men among the private families of an intelligent and refined community, and hence this policy has been adopted."

Minds changed the next decade. West Side Row, built in 1886 and 1887, comprised six brick cottages, of which five yet stand. Each housed sixteen students—two to a room, four rooms to a floor, two floors to a cottage, every room with a corner fireplace and outside entrance.

West Side Hall was built in 1887 to provide dining facilities for these dormitories.

Students named the six identical cottages in West Side Row Alpha, Belleview, Cumberland, Delphi, Euclid, and Franklin in alphabetical order from West End. They were converted to apartments in the 1940s.

Left: West Side Hall has had four lives—dining hall for West Side Row; home of the campus YMCA; college classrooms; and, since 1945, headquarters of the Naval ROTC unit.

William Henry Vanderbilt (left), the Commodore's son and principal heir, followed his father in command of the New York Central Railroad and in concern for the University. He gave the money to build old Wesley, Science Hall, and the old Gymnasium. His oldest son Cornelius II paid for Mechanical Engineering Hall, which was the first building placed toward the foot of the hill. The decorative governor still on its roof (right) symbolized mechanical force. It was the Age of Steam.

William C. Smith was architect for Mechanical Engineering Hall, erected in 1888, the first building in Tennessee designed for teaching of engineering. It also produced steam to heat other campus buildings and, from 1899 until about 1918, electricity to light them. In 1965 the building became headquarters for the Army ROTC.

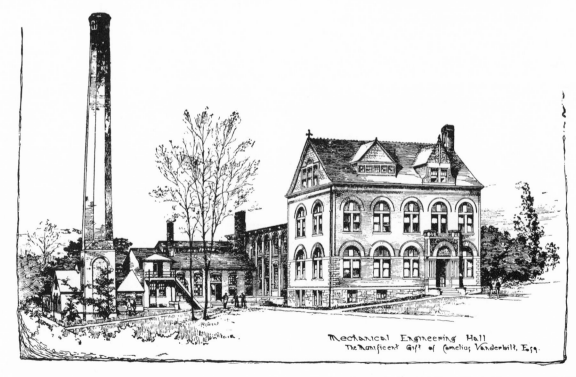

Mechanical Engineering Hall
The Munificent Gift of Cornelius Vanderbilt, Esq.

1890s 🙠 A place to learn, a place to live, a place to play

State Capitol is on horizon at left, Tarbox School is big building in center of this picture, taken from a Vanderbilt building in 1888.

Opposite page: 1897 map by Granbery Jackson, Instructor in Drawing.

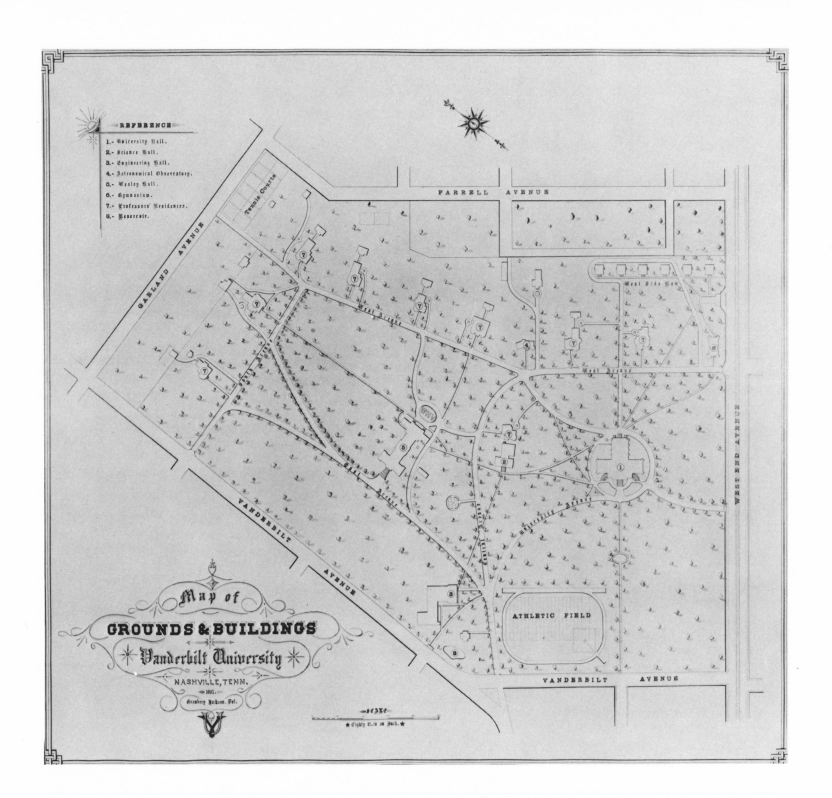

REFERENCE

1.– University Hall.
2.– Science Hall.
3.– Engineering Hall.
4.– Astronomical Observatory.
5.– Wesley Hall.
6.– Gymnasium.
7.– Professors' Residences.
8.– Reservoir.

FARRELL AVENUE

GARLAND AVENUE

Temple Courts

West Side Row

West Avenue

West Avenue

VANDERBILT AVENUE

WEST END AVENUE

ATHLETIC FIELD

VANDERBILT AVENUE

Map of
GROUNDS & BUILDINGS
Vanderbilt University
NASHVILLE, TENN.
1897.
Stanbery Jackson. Del.

SCALE

Eighty ft. to an Inch.

Broad Street ended and the campus began at this iron gate. Two others swung like this one between stone pillars on West End Avenue at the Gymnasium and on Hillsboro Road at Edgehill. A board fence enclosed the campus. Gates were locked at night and on Sundays to preserve privacy and to exclude livestock that grazed on nearby commons.

It was in the 1890s that the extra-curricular aspects of college life became important at Vanderbilt. The preceding decade saw the University abandon its rules against dormitories, fraternities, theater-going, etc., and saw the birth of the annual *Comet* and the weekly *Hustler*. The Glee Club sang its first concert in 1891. The 1895 catalogue announced admission of women as regular students; they previously were suffered but scarcely recognized. Baseball, track, and football flourished, and basketball was introduced in 1893 only fifteen months after that game was invented. In 1895 Vanderbilt's Dr. William L. Dudley, Professor of Chemistry and Dean of Medicine, organized the Southern Intercollegiate Athletic Association. Dudley Field is named for him.

The academic side stayed strong. Tennessee Alpha chapter of Phi Beta Kappa was chartered in 1901.

"*Vaaaanderbilt stile!*" was the streetcar conductor's cry
when his trolley slowed for a stop here, on West End Avenue
abreast of the Main Building. The first electric cars came
in 1889. In 1874, when the cornerstone of the Main Building
was laid, the cars were pulled by mules or horses, and the
new university was at the end of the line.

Time to gather the hay.

Right: High-wheeled "ordinary" bicycle in center was giving way to the new "safety" models in 1892 when this photo of the Bicycle Club was made at the Main Building.

Below: Football at Vanderbilt began in 1890 but this 1891 team, pictured on the Main Building steps, was the first to play a regular schedule—four games, home-and-away against Washington University and Sewanee.

Lower right: The Tennis House's gallery for spectators overlooked the courts that were on Garland Avenue from the 1880s until ousted in 1963 by doctors' parking lot.

Opposite page: This picture was taken during the first baseball game played on the new athletic field, called Dudley until 1922, Curry Field since then. The year was 1892, Vanderbilt at bat against Cumberland University.

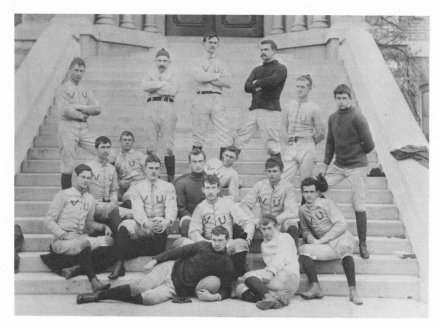

1902 ❧ 'A plan providing for all future buildings'

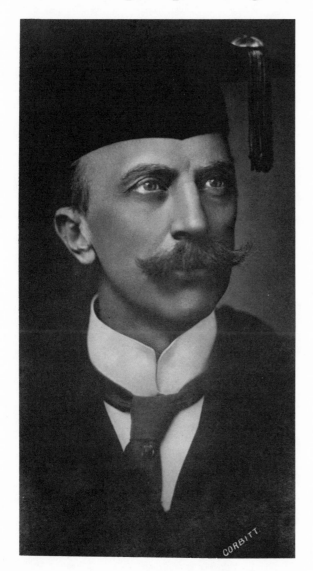

James H. Kirkland, a South Carolinian, earned his Ph.D. at Leipzig, came to Vanderbilt as Professor of Latin in 1886, and was elected Chancellor in 1893 at age 33. He was the University's chief executive 44 years, retiring in 1937.

At the turn of the century, the Commodore's grandson William Kissam Vanderbilt provided Kissam Hall in memory of his mother. The architects were Hunt & Hunt, the firm responsible for W. K. Vanderbilt's own mansion in New York and the splendid houses of his brothers, Cornelius's "The Breakers" in Newport, Rhode Island, and George's "Biltmore" in Asheville, North Carolina.

After Kissam Hall was completed, Chancellor Kirkland asked Hunt & Hunt to study the campus and propose a plan for the whole. In 1902 Kirkland reported to the Board of Trust that—

"As a result of this study they have made a plan providing for all future buildings that may at any time be placed on our campus. This gives us a definite plan toward which we may work, and prevents the location of a building at any time in an unsuitable place. Every institution looking to a large future ought to have made a plan of this kind, and it would have been well if this work had been done for Vanderbilt earlier in our history. It is true that no very serious mistakes have been made, but some changes will ultimately be required. Science Hall, standing as it does in the center of the grounds, gives place on the Hunt & Hunt plan to a large library building . . ."

Main feature of the Hunt & Hunt plan was the entrance facing Broadway, leading straight up the hill to the library that was never built there.

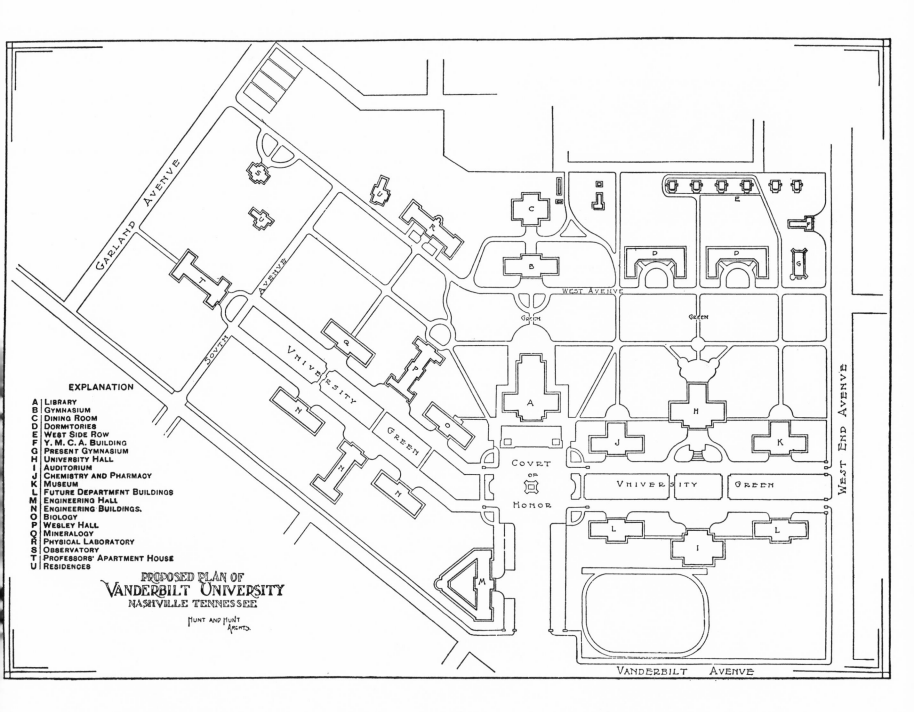

EXPLANATION

A | LIBRARY
B | GYMNASIUM
C | DINING ROOM
D | DORMITORIES
E | WEST SIDE ROW
F | Y. M. C. A. BUILDING
G | PRESENT GYMNASIUM
H | UNIVERSITY HALL
I | AUDITORIUM
J | CHEMISTRY AND PHARMACY
K | MUSEUM
L | FUTURE DEPARTMENT BUILDINGS
M | ENGINEERING HALL
N | ENGINEERING BUILDINGS.
O | BIOLOGY
P | WESLEY HALL
Q | MINERALOGY
R | PHYSICAL LABORATORY
S | OBSERVATORY
T | PROFESSORS' APARTMENT HOUSE
U | RESIDENCES

PROPOSED PLAN OF
VANDERBILT UNIVERSITY
NASHVILLE TENNESSEE

HUNT AND HUNT
ARCHTS.

55

Kissam Hall, 1901—1958

The March 1901 issue of *Vanderbilt University Quarterly* said of Kissam Hall:
"While constructed of materials and in a style not dissimilar to the other
buildings, it is superior to them all in architectural beauty. . . ."
The view below is from about 1910. At the left is the domed Observatory.
The long building in the middle distance near the picture's righthand edge
is the Hippodrome roller skating rink. Biggest expanse of vacant land beyond
Kissam's cupolas became the site of the Stadium and Memorial Gymnasium.

The cafeteria in the basement of Kissam Hall,
shown here in the early 1950s, was the main
provider of meals for students from 1901 until
1954, when its function was taken over by Rand Hall.

Left: Kissam in horse-and-buggy days, and typical floor plan. Most of 200 men in Kissam occupied two-man suites with a common study flanked by separate bedrooms. Baths were in the basement. Note on pronunciation: Accent second syllable of Kissam, notwithstanding the popular motto of its libertine residents, "Kiss 'em all."

Below: Wooden fire escapes were added on back as safeguards for the students crowded into Kissam in the years immediately after World War II. To modernize the old dorm would have cost too much, and it was razed in 1958, a year after its replacement, Kissam Quadrangle, was completed. Its removal created Alumni Lawn.

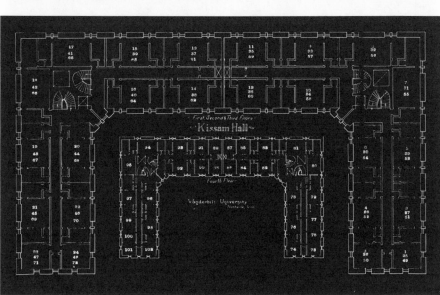

57

Electricity . . . This steam-driven generator, or "dynamo" as it was called, was installed in Mechanical Engineering Hall in 1898. It produced the power for electric lights on campus the next year.

Automobile . . .   About 1900, engineering students in the machine shop worked on this primitive automobile. The 1902 plan for the campus did not anticipate effects of electricity and automobiles.

1905 ❧ The Plan Refined (for a while)

Mrs. Francis Furman bequeathed to Vanderbilt money for a building in memory of her husband, a Nashville merchant. The University had to decide where to place it and had misgivings about the 1902 plan of Hunt & Hunt. Help was sought from George Kessler, a Kansas City landscape architect acclaimed for his layout of the 1903 St. Louis Exposition. The Kessler plan for Vanderbilt refined the plan of Hunt & Hunt and determined the site of Furman Hall (*'H' in the drawing opposite*).

That was the one and only effect of the Kessler plan. Instead of the elaborate court that it proposed for the slope upward from Broadway, the University made do with a plain road and a pair of stone gateposts. And, as the years went by, Vanderbilt rejected Kessler's negative view of old Science, old Central, the old Gym, West Side Row, and the faculty residences, all of which the 1905 Kessler plan would have demolished.

Furman Hall was built in 1907 in the style of a stone castle to complement the battlements of the reconstructed Main Building, its near neighbor. It was for Chemistry; the photograph at left shows a laboratory full of students in the 1920s. Above is the facade as it looked before it acquired different roofline in 1967.

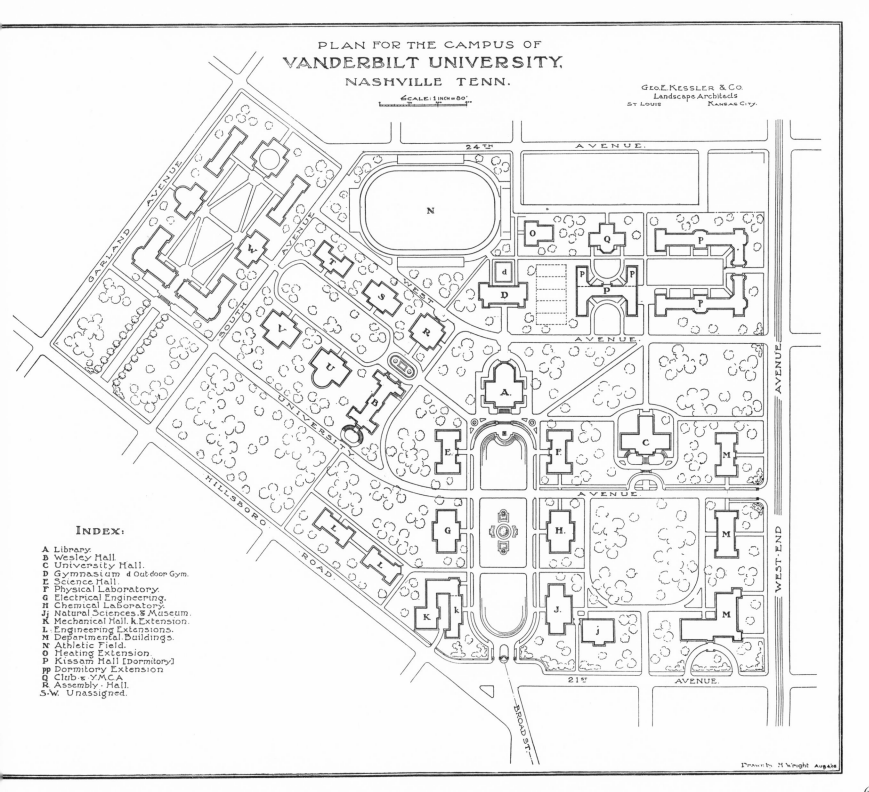

PLAN FOR THE CAMPUS OF
VANDERBILT UNIVERSITY,
NASHVILLE TENN.

SCALE: 1 INCH = 80'

Geo. E. Kessler & Co.
Landscape Architects
ST LOUIS   KANSAS CITY.

INDEX:

A Library.
B Wesley Hall.
C University Hall.
D Gymnasium d Out-door Gym.
E Science Hall.
F Physical Laboratory.
G Electrical Engineering.
H Chemical Laboratory.
Jj Natural Sciences.& Museum.
K Mechanical Hall. k.Extension.
L Engineering Extensions.
M Departmental Buildings.
N Athletic Field.
O Heating Extension.
P Kissam Hall [Dormitory]
pp Dormitory Extension
Q Club.& Y.M.C.A.
R Assembly · Hall.
S·W· Unassigned.

Drawn by H. Wright Aug 4.05

After the Chemistry Department abandoned Furman Hall in 1964 for new and larger quarters in Stevenson Center for the Natural Sciences, Furman stayed vacant while the University pondered whether to tear it down. Finally and fortunately, the preservationists' arguments prevailed. In 1967 the interior spaces were successfully remodeled to house the humanities, including philosophy and the foreign language departments. Old brick walls, stripped of plaster, are featured. The photograph opposite shows the view from just inside the front door.

Compare the picture above with one on page 50; the stone gateposts have been moved farther apart for automobiles. Furman Hall is beyond bleacher seats at the old football field's south end, where the Law School is now. Road is gone but the gateposts are still there *(upper right)*.

James H. Alley—Cap Alley in life and legend—was the one-man police force, beginning in 1887 and active until a short time before he died May 31, 1927.

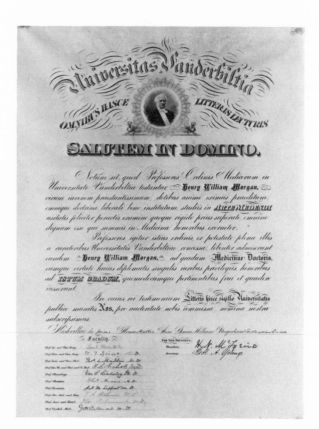

South Campus

Diplomas at left—University of Nashville above, Vanderbilt below—bear the same date, March 1, 1875, and certify the same degree, Doctor of Medicine, awarded the same man, Henry William Morgan. The coincidence illustrates the origin of the Vanderbilt School of Medicine. In 1874 the trustees simply recognized the existing medical school of the University of Nashville as the medical school of their university also. Students took their choice of diplomas or paid extra and got both, as did Dr. Morgan, who was the first man to be handed a Vanderbilt diploma of any kind.

Nashville's diploma depicts the building of Greek Revival style that housed the one school that, from 1874 to 1895, had two names. It stood south of Broad in the block bounded by Market and College streets (now Second and Third), Franklin, and what is now Peabody Street. The building is gone; the block has been a public park since 1913. The school, while nominally a department of the two universities, was the responsibility of local physicians, educationally and financially. The course of study was two years of five months each.

Vanderbilt quit that arrangement in 1895, took responsibility for its own medical department, housed it in a new building on the southeast corner of Summer (now Fifth) and Elm streets, and introduced the South's first four-year medical curriculum. The University of Nashville's medical department eventually disappeared by merger with the University of Tennessee.

Meanwhile, a third institution came on scene. This was Peabody, which evolved from State Normal College and inherited the University of Nashville's main campus, a 16-acre tract between Middleton and Lindsley avenues. In 1911 Peabody traded it to Vanderbilt, and Vanderbilt moved its schools of Medicine and Dentistry into the old buildings in 1912. South Campus, so called because it was in South Nashville, served the School of Medicine until it came to Twenty-first and Garland in 1925.

From left to right in this panoramic view of South Campus are the School of Dentistry, Business Office, Gymnasium, and School of Medicine. In the excerpt from 1879 map of Nashville, Vanderbilt is at lower left and University of Nashville is at the right center near the river.

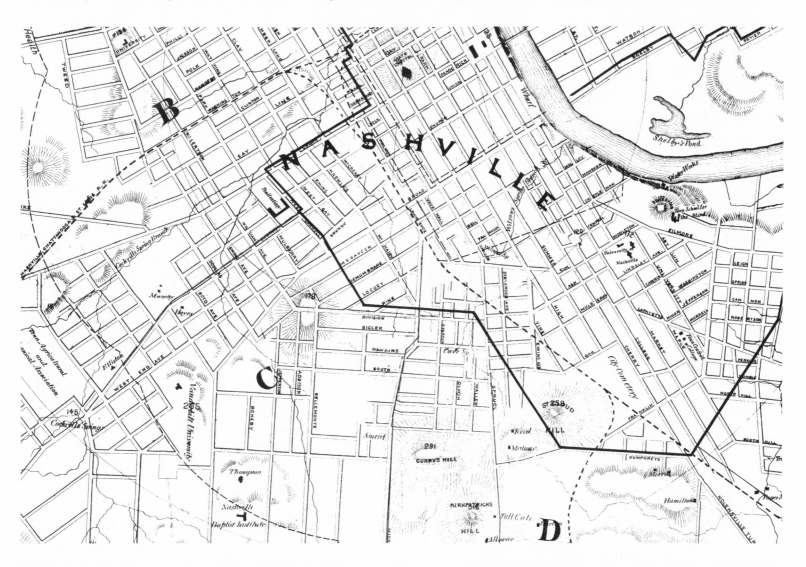

Three Survivors.

This building and two on the opposite page survive from the old South Campus, this one remodeled in 1978-79 as offices for the Metropolitan Nashville Planning Commission and its staff. It was built in 1853-54 for the University of Nashville and was designed by Adolphus Heiman, Nashville architect whose proposal for the Tennessee State Capitol was second to William Strickland's classic design.

It was the birthplace of Montgomery Bell Academy (1867), George Peabody College for Teachers (1875), and the Cumberland Museum (1945). It also housed Western Military Institute (1856—), a Union Army hospital (1862—), the Medical School of Vanderbilt University (1912-1925), the Tennessee National Guard (1932—), and the Tennessee State Guard (1943—).

Vanderbilt acquired it in 1911 from Peabody along with the other buildings and land within the South Campus's principal block—bounded on north and south by Middleton and Lindsley avenues, on east and west by University Street and Second Avenue.

The Medical School moved to the main campus in 1925. The School of Dentistry remained on South Campus until 1926 and then was discontinued.

Vanderbilt sold the block of land and buildings in 1939 for $100,000 to the City of Nashville, which wanted the site to build Howard High School.

In 1916 Methodists of the Nashville area began to build Galloway Memorial Hospital on South Campus as an affiliate of the School of Medicine, but could not complete the structure when only half the pledges were paid. For more than twenty years it stood unfinished and empty, as in this picture. The City of Nashville eventually converted most of the yellow brick shell to the Metro Office Building.

This is Second Avenue in 1978, the stone wall of old South Campus on the right. Across the street is the building erected about 1900 by the medical department of University of Nashville. In 1915 it became Litterer Laboratory of Vanderbilt School of Medicine by gift from Mr. William Litterer, a Nashville philanthropist.

Left: This was the building Vanderbilt constructed in 1895 for its own School of Medicine (called Medical Department then) after quitting its affiliation with the University of Nashville. It was on the southeast corner of Fifth and Elm, and was turned into a hospital and dispensary in 1915. The building was razed in the 1930s because it stood in the way of the extension of Lafayette Street and U.S. highway 41.

Elsewhere in the City . . .

In the fall of 1889 Vanderbilt schools of Dentistry and Law moved into their new stone building depicted in the woodcut at right. It was on the west side of Fourth Avenue, North, midway between Union and Deaderick streets, and in later years it became better known as the home of the Chamber of Commerce. It was razed in 1970; the Raddison Hotel was rising on the site in 1978.

The Dental School's earliest home, from 1880 to 1889, was at the corner of Broad and High (Sixth). From 1901 to 1912 it was on Ninth near Broad, and from 1912 until discontinued in 1926 it was on South Campus.

Law School began in October 1874 on College Street (Third) in a rented room over the Fourth National Bank. It was housed on the campus in the Main Building from 1875 to 1889 and again from 1916 to 1962. Its location downtown during the twenty-five year interim was a convenience for the faculty, who were downtown lawyers.

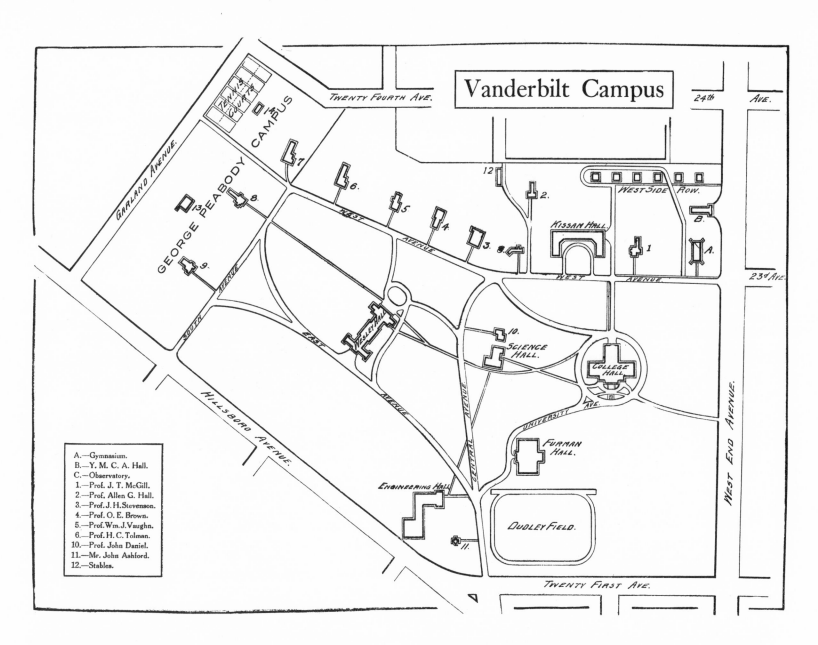

Vanderbilt Campus

Map legend:
- A.—Gymnasium.
- B.—Y. M. C. A. Hall.
- C.—Observatory.
- 1.—Prof. J. T. McGill.
- 2.—Prof. Allen G. Hall.
- 3.—Prof. J. H. Stevenson.
- 4.—Prof. O. E. Brown.
- 5.—Prof. Wm. J. Vaughn.
- 6.—Prof. H. C. Tolman.
- 10.—Prof. John Daniel.
- 11.—Mr. John Ashford.
- 12.—Stables.

Note the label, George Peabody Campus, next to Garland Avenue on map from Vanderbilt's 1913 catalogue. Vanderbilt got South Campus when it deeded this plot of about 12 acres to Peabody in 1911, expecting Peabody to locate its buildings here. Instead Peabody bought more land across Hillsboro for its campus. To get back the plot—which in time became the Medical Center site—Vanderbilt bought and conveyed to Peabody in 1914 land on which Peabody built its Demonstration School (later University School of Nashville).

1920s ✌ A New Plan for a Unified University

Pictured above while under construction, the
School of Medicine and Vanderbilt University Hospital
opened in 1925, first in the United States to join under
one roof a medical school's departmental laboratories
and its teaching hospital. The building under way
on the right is the School of Nursing.

Vast change came in the 1920s. First, Vanderbilt leaped over two westward blocks to reach vacant land on which to build what was then the South's largest stadium, seating 20,000. And Vanderbilt decided to abandon its other campus in South Nashville and unify its School of Medicine with the rest of the University. To build an entirely new medical plant required an entirely new plan for the campus, and Vanderbilt got it from Day & Klauder, Philadelphia architects who had served Yale, Johns Hopkins, and other universities. The Day & Klauder plan was completed in 1924 and, unlike it predecessors, respected the contours of the land. Its influence was enormous. It determined the sites of the School of Medicine and the Hospital, the School of Nursing, the Power House, Alumni Memorial Hall, Neely Auditorium, Buttrick, Calhoun, Garland, McGill and Tolman—the last two shifted slightly to save West Side Row rather than old Kissam. The Day & Klauder plan made the best of Furman's odd location by proposing a new entrance, never built, to its rear. The plan also assumed old Science Hall would be razed.

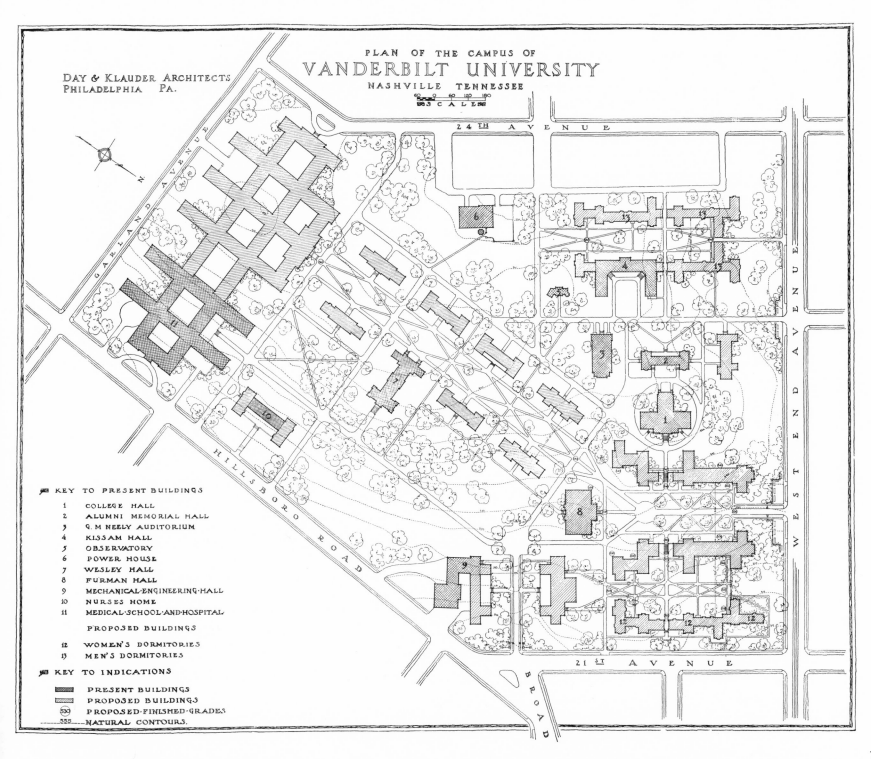

PLAN OF THE CAMPUS OF
VANDERBILT UNIVERSITY
NASHVILLE TENNESSEE

DAY & KLAUDER ARCHITECTS
PHILADELPHIA PA.

KEY TO PRESENT BUILDINGS

1 COLLEGE HALL
2 ALUMNI MEMORIAL HALL
3 Q. M. NEELY AUDITORIUM
4 KISSAM HALL
5 OBSERVATORY
6 POWER HOUSE
7 WESLEY HALL
8 FURMAN HALL
9 MECHANICAL ENGINEERING HALL
10 NURSES HOME
11 MEDICAL SCHOOL AND HOSPITAL

PROPOSED BUILDINGS

12 WOMEN'S DORMITORIES
13 MEN'S DORMITORIES

KEY TO INDICATIONS

PRESENT BUILDINGS
PROPOSED BUILDINGS
PROPOSED FINISHED GRADES
NATURAL CONTOURS.

Collegiate Gothic.

Collegiate Gothic architecture came to the campus
in 1925 with the new Medical School, designed by
Henry R. Shepley, of Coolidge & Shattuck, Boston,
and especially with Alumni Memorial Hall *(right)*
and Neely Auditorium, both by Henry C. Hibbs, who
had come to Nashville in 1914 as resident manager
for Ludlow & Peabody, the architects for the Peabody
campus. Hibbs also designed Buttrick, Calhoun, and
Garland halls for Vanderbilt, the Y.M.C.A. Graduate School
that later became new Wesley Hall, the Joint University
Libraries' main building, and Scarritt College.

Alumni Memorial Hall was the student center until Rand and Sarratt took over that function. It was gradually converted to offices.

Stadium.

In 1922 it was the South's largest, with capacity of 20,000
when it was dedicated at the game in which Vanderbilt tied
Michigan 0-0. The photograph below shows it in 1930 overflowing
for the Tennessee game, lost, alas, to the visitors 13-0
on Bobby Dodd's two touchdown passes to Buddy Hackman.

Names of forty-four Vanderbilt men who lost their lives in World War I are carved on the mantels in the Memorial Room.

The pool room in the south basement of Alumni offered an escape from studies for thirty years. The tables are now in Sarratt.

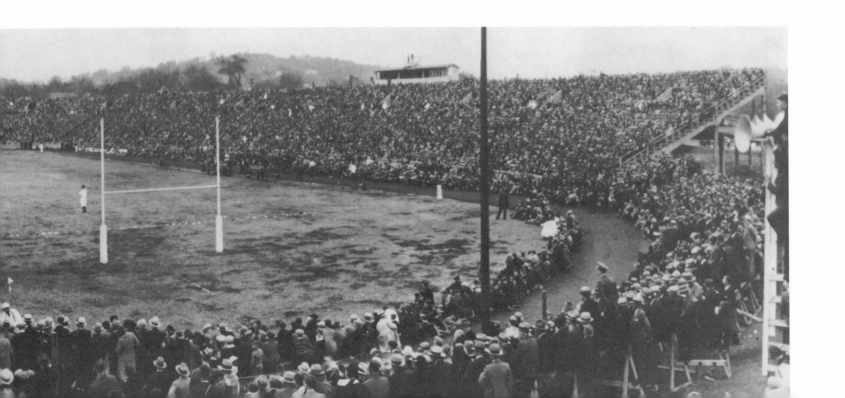

When Neely Auditorium was new in 1925, its pews for 1,100 could seat all the undergraduate students and their teachers.

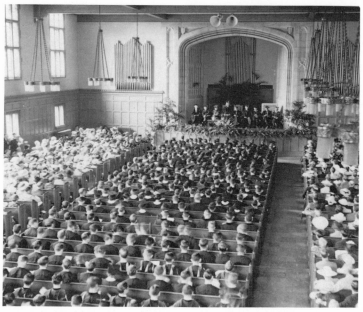

Vanderbilt's graduation exercises were conducted in Neely from 1925 through 1948, after which they were moved outdoors.

This gate of varicolored stone was a Class of 1922 project for the Twenty-third Avenue entrance. It stood there about 30 years.

Neely's interior was converted to a versatile theater. Here is the set for the opener, *A Streetcar Named Desire*, in November 1976.

In 1928 Buttrick *(above)*, Garland, and Calhoun halls kept liberal arts from being overshadowed by Medical School's new eminence.

Buttrick *(left)* housed Biology then and now. Garland *(above)* was the home of Physics until 1964 and of Geology until 1979.

Calhoun Hall provided an assortment of classrooms and offices for the College, principally the social sciences and humanities.

Bookstore was inside this door at the lower end of Calhoun Hall for twenty years, 1928 to 1948. This picture is from 1944/45.

1940s ❧ The Effects of Fire, Depression, and War

This aerial photograph of the campus and adjacent neighborhoods was made between 1928 and 1932, a period of no visible changes.

Wesley Hall in flames February 19, 1932, 5:15 p.m.

The University long lacked means to raze the ruins.

Vanderbilt's official portrait
of Chancellor Carmichael.

Old Wesley Hall burned February 19, 1932. The calamity occurred at the very depth of the Great Depression. The combination of events halted thought of future growth—and changed, for better and worse, the plans for campus development.

Where old Wesley was, we have the Library Lawn. Bricks from its walls were used in 1940 to build McTyeire Hall, Vanderbilt's first dormitory for women other than nurses. McTyeire provided rooms for 100, a number then considered sufficient for all time. The dormitory was placed in the way of Medical Center expansion.

In those times the idea of the Joint University Libraries was conceived, and pushed forward by Oliver Cromwell Carmichael, Chancellor from 1937 to 1946. Ground that old Wesley had faced was available for the main library building, dedicated December 5 and 6, 1941, the two days before the Japanese bombed Pearl Harbor.

Library Lawn.

Removal of the ruins of old Wesley Hall created the largest open space on campus and provided attractive sites for the General Library at the far end of the photograph opposite, the Divinity School on the left, and Stevenson Center for the Natural Sciences off camera to the right. The bronze statue of Harold Stirling Vanderbilt portrays him in his academic role as President of the Board of Trust, an office he filled with force for thirteen years.

Right: Commencement on Library Lawn, June 2, 1963. Outdoor Commencements were here, 1949 through 1969.

This was the original facade of the General Library building of the Joint University Libraries, facing Twenty-first Avenue.

In vivid contrast to Collegiate Gothic, the H. Fort Flowers Graduate Wing was added to the front of the Library in 1969.

79

Years 1880 and 1936 on Wesley Hall facade were when old Wesley was built and when this one was acquired by the University.

More about two of these—

The building at left faces the General Library from across Twenty-first Avenue. Completed in 1928, it was originally the Y.M.C.A. Graduate School, designed for the training of Y.M.C.A. secretaries. Vanderbilt used its gymnasiums and swimming pool for physical education classes, and in 1936 took over the building as a home for the Divinity School.

The building below was originally a plain two-story brick house built in the 1880s by the Misses Parnell, who pastured cows where Branscomb Quadrangle is now. Miss Patti Parnell conducted a private elementary school, called ''Little Vanderbilt'' by Bishop McTyeire, for children of faculty. In the early 1920s the Kirk Rankin family remodeled the house in Mediterranean style, unusual in Nashville. Vanderbilt bought it as a home for the Chancellor—Carmichael from 1940 to 1946, Branscomb from 1946 until 1953, when a larger house on Harding Road was acquired. From 1953 to 1962 it housed the AOPi sorority, the University Club from 1962 to 1969, and since then the Undergraduate Admissions Office.

Bricks from old Wesley built McTyeire Hall in 1940 on a site that the Day & Klauder plan *(page 71)* reserved for Medical expansion.

Mediterranean style of 401 24th dates from early 1920s remodeling of an 1880s house, Vanderbilt Chancellors lived here, 1940 to 1953.

Inscribed cornerstone of old Kissam Hall is set into the wall of Tolman Hall *(above)*, modern dormitory nearest the old one's site.

Six temporary buildings put in 1946 on Garland Avenue contained twenty-eight small apartments for World War II married veterans.

McGill Hall, as well as Tolman, was completed in 1947 and helped house veterans who were more than half of all students enrolled.

Naval ROTC band in parade formation on Curry Field in 1949/50, when fraternities occupied two of the houses in the background.

Edward Stone's plan for the campus, in perspective from the north. West End Avenue runs diagonally across picture to lower right corner.

arvie Branscomb was Chancellor from 1946 until 1963. The number of buildings undertaken during his administration surpassed the number that were on campus when he came. For a master plan, he called on Edward Durell Stone, internationally known New York architect. Stone's 1947 plan shifted the main entrance to West End Avenue, in fact proposed extending the entrance drive to the high ground now occupied by Stevenson Center, where he thought a dominant chapel might be. He put the Engineering School (1950) and Rand Hall (1953) where they blocked the old road that had been a busy thoroughfare from West End to Garland Avenue. He recommended placing as many buildings as practicable on the perimeter of the campus to screen the interior from the noise and commotion of city streets.

Vanderbilt's official portrait of Harvie Branscomb.

The first academic addition to the campus after World War II was new home for School of Engineering (1950).

83

Memorial Gymnasium commemorates Vanderbilt men and women who served in the armed forces during World War II. The view at right is from across the baseball field when it was under construction. Upper picture on opposite page was taken the night of the first game, December 6, 1952, during dedication ceremony. Seating capacity then was 6,000. Two balconies on each side and the extensions on east and west ends were added later as demand grew.

Nearest picture shows Memorial Gymnasium completed with the soaring wings added onto the ends in 1969. Balconies on sides were added in 1965 and 1967. Its capacity of 15,528 spectators made it third largest on any campus. Picture on opposite page shows a typical full house for a Southeastern Conference basketball game.

Vanderbilt Theater was built in 1948, using mainly
war surplus materials provided by the Federal
Works Agency, and was considered temporary from
the start. It seated 429 in plain surroundings.
The stage was commodious, as shown here. The building
was razed in 1975 to clear the Garland Avenue site
for Rudolph A. Light Hall for medical education.

Below: Cole Hall before it
was finished in 1949.

Below: Twin dormitories joined together, Frederick Vanderbilt and
Barnard halls opened in 1952, last of the Collegiate Gothic style.

Kissam Quadrangle's six dormitories, each housing 100 men, were opened in 1957. Beyond on left and right are St. Thomas Hospital and the tower of the Cathedral of the Incarnation, and the State Capitol and other downtown buildings farther away. In the 1970s Kissam ceased being for men only, as Branscomb ceased being for women only.

Right: Inside the quad, snow falling.

Above: Rand Hall's north facade and its main
dining room in 1954. It opened in January of that year.

Left:
The Wall at Rand, September 1978,
place to sun, see, and be seen.

On a hill six miles south of the campus and 500 feet higher, Arthur J. Dyer Observatory in 1953 was an early extension of the campus.

Seyfert Telescope, a 24-inch reflector, was named for the professor of astronomy who inspired and directed the research facility.

This photograph was used almost twenty years,
1958 through 1976, in the front of catalogues of
the College of Arts and Science because it por-
trayed Kirkland Tower and conveyed a feeling
of tranquility that the inner campus retained
during a period of much building. The map also was used throughout that period, updated
every year or so. The 1958 first edition is reproduced here. The Divinity School was included because it was under construction.

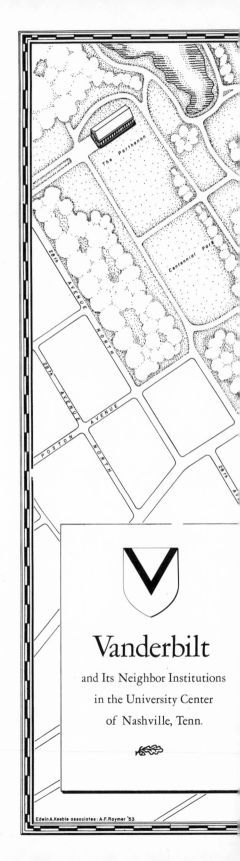

Vanderbilt

and Its Neighbor Institutions

in the University Center

of Nashville, Tenn.

Edwin A. Keeble associates: A.F. Raymer '53

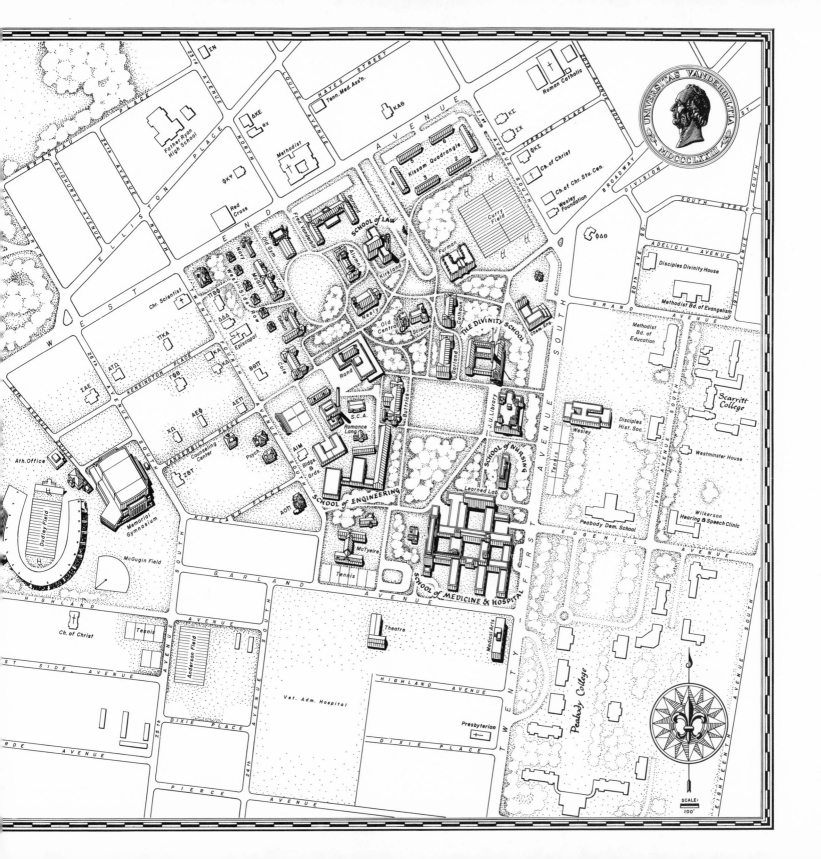

Divinity School quadrangle from Library
Lawn, at left, and Benton Chapel, above,
from the campus side of the Library.

"Word of God" window of the chapel, above, as seen from the balcony, and the interior as seen from behind the pulpit.

Benton Chapel is the richest building at Vanderbilt in symbolic architectural details. Notice the three crosses high on its rear wall; they are formed by bricks extending slightly beyond the others and are highlighted by the early morning sun in this photograph. Two archangels in bronze—Gabriel with trumpet and Michael with sword—are handles for the front doors of the chapel. The Divinity School quadrangle was completed in 1959. Its architects were Brush, Hutchison & Gwinn, of Nashville.

The School of Law, quartered upstairs in Kirkland since 1915, got its own building in 1962. It also was designed by Brush, Hutchison & Gwinn.

Law School Library.

Refreshments in the atrium.

Faculty Assembly in Underwood Auditorium, August 31, 1978.

High-rise Lewis *(directly ahead)* and Morgan houses provided apartments for married students in 1962, year Law School was finished.

The Campus Extended

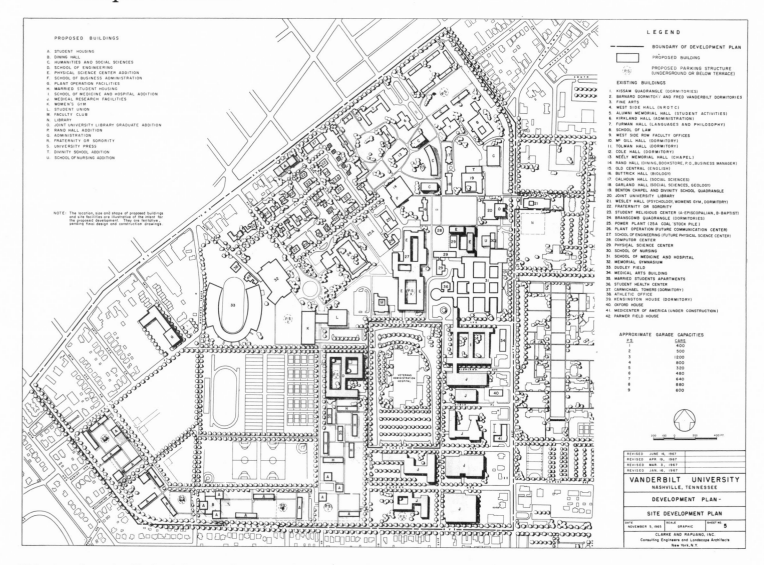

PROPOSED BUILDINGS

A. STUDENT HOUSING
B. DINING HALL
C. HUMANITIES AND SOCIAL SCIENCES
D. SCHOOL OF ENGINEERING
E. PHYSICAL SCIENCE CENTER ADDITION
F. SCHOOL OF BUSINESS ADMINISTRATION
G. PLANT OPERATION FACILITIES
H. MARRIED STUDENT HOUSING
J. SCHOOL OF MEDICINE AND HOSPITAL ADDITION
J. MEDICAL RESEARCH FACILITIES
K. WOMEN'S GYM
L. STUDENT UNION
M. FACULTY CLUB
N. LIBRARY
O. JOINT UNIVERSITY LIBRARY GRADUATE ADDITION
P. RAND HALL ADDITION
Q. ADMINISTRATION
R. FRATERNITY OR SORORITY
S. UNIVERSITY PRESS
T. DIVINITY SCHOOL ADDITION
U. SCHOOL OF NURSING ADDITION

NOTE: The location, size and shape of proposed buildings and site facilities are illustrative of the intent for the proposed development. They are tentative, pending final design and construction drawings.

LEGEND

— — — BOUNDARY OF DEVELOPMENT PLAN

▢ PROPOSED BUILDING

PROPOSED PARKING STRUCTURE (UNDERGROUND OR BELOW TERRACE)

EXISTING BUILDINGS

1. KISSAM QUADRANGLE (DORMITORIES)
2. BARNARD DORMITORY AND FRED VANDERBILT DORMITORIES
3. FINE ARTS
4. WEST SIDE HALL (NROTC)
5. ALUMNI MEMORIAL HALL (STUDENT ACTIVITIES)
6. KIRKLAND HALL (ADMINISTRATION)
7. FURMAN HALL (LANGUAGES AND PHILOSOPHY)
8. SCHOOL OF LAW
9. WEST SIDE ROW FACULTY OFFICES
10. Mc GILL HALL (DORMITORY)
11. TOLMAN HALL (DORMITORY)
12. COLE HALL (DORMITORY)
13. NEELY MEMORIAL HALL (CHAPEL)
14. RAND HALL (DINING, BOOKSTORE, P.O., BUSINESS MANAGER)
15. OLD CENTRAL (ENGLISH)
16. BUTTRICK HALL (BIOLOGY)
17. CALHOUN HALL (SOCIAL SCIENCES)
18. GARLAND HALL (SOCIAL SCIENCES, GEOLOGY)
19. BENTON CHAPEL AND DIVINITY SCHOOL QUADRANGLE
20. JOINT UNIVERSITY LIBRARY
21. WESLEY HALL (PSYCHOLOGY, WOMENS GYM, DORMITORY)
22. FRATERNITY OR SORORITY
23. STUDENT RELIGIOUS CENTER (A-EPISCOPALIAN, B-BAPTIST)
24. BRANSCOMB QUADRANGLE (DORMITORIES)
25. POWER PLANT (25A COAL STOCK PILE)
26. PLANT OPERATION (FUTURE COMMUNICATION CENTER)
27. SCHOOL OF ENGINEERING (FUTURE PHYSICAL SCIENCE CENTER)
28. COMPUTOR CENTER
29. PHYSICAL SCIENCE CENTER
30. SCHOOL OF NURSING
31. SCHOOL OF MEDICINE AND HOSPITAL
32. MEMORIAL GYMNASIUM
33. DUDLEY FIELD
34. MEDICAL ARTS BUILDING
35. MARRIED STUDENTS APARTMENTS
36. STUDENT HEALTH CENTER
37. CARMICHAEL TOWERS (DORMITORY)
38. ATHLETIC OFFICE
39. KENSINGTON HOUSE (DORMITORY)
40. OXFORD HOUSE
41. MEDICENTER OF AMERICA (UNDER CONSTRUCTION)
42. PARMER FIELD HOUSE

APPROXIMATE GARAGE CAPACITIES

P.S.	CARS
1	400
2	500
3	1200
4	800
5	320
6	480
7	640
8	880
9	600

REVISED	JUNE 16, 1967
REVISED	APR. 19, 1967
REVISED	MAR. 3, 1967
REVISED	JAN. 16, 1967

VANDERBILT UNIVERSITY
NASHVILLE, TENNESSEE

DEVELOPMENT PLAN -

SITE DEVELOPMENT PLAN

DATE	SCALE	SHEET NO.
NOVEMBER 5, 1965	GRAPHIC	5

CLARKE AND RAPUANO, INC.
Consulting Engineers and Landscape Architects
New York, N.Y.

This plan, drawn by Clarke & Rapuano in 1965 (updated to 1967), projected development of the campus southward to Blakemore and southwestward to Thirty-first. Terms of the University Center Urban Renewal Project required Vanderbilt to buy 501 parcels of real estate and to clear the land of the houses that were there, looking toward the area's upgrading by its development for educational and educationally related purposes. The campus thus doubled in area and by the late 1970s included about 260 acres.

Clarke & Rapuano, New York engineers and landscape architects, were employed by Vanderbilt because of work the firm was doing for the City of Nashville in regard to urban renewal. Their 1965 plan was the first to extend the campus to Blakemore and Thirty-first avenues—its southern and southwestern boundaries in the University Center Urban Renewal Project.

By then nearly everybody recognized that all too little space was left on the original campus, that what remained should be reserved for essential educational purposes, and that tall buildings use less land. Clarke & Rapuano proposed to meet residential needs in areas purchased to the south and southwest, and this had been done in the case of Lewis and Morgan houses (1962). The difficulty was that whole blocks of older private dwellings in that direction could not be acquired as fast as the student body grew during the booming '60s. Consequently, Carmichael Towers were put on West End Avenue, two at a time in 1966 and 1970, as those lots were available.

Above: Looking northeast across the intersection of Natchez Trace and Blakemore Avenue in 1978. Blakemore had been newly widened to five lanes.

Right: Parklike appearance in 1978 of land cleared of houses but not of trees in triangle formed by Thirty-first, Vanderbilt Place, and Natchez Trace. The view is from Thirty-first, looking east.

Above: The old Phi Delta Theta house on Broadway faced campus entrance. It was built in 1910. The chapter organized sub rosa in 1876, the first fraternity at Vanderbilt.
Upper right: Old Tri Delta house on Twenty-fourth faced Kensington Place. These two pictures are from 1927.

Memorial Gymnasium and the other athletic facilities were separated from the campus proper by several blocks of residences that the University began acquiring after World War II. The area became an integral part of the campus in the 1960s when Branscomb Quadrangle and a new fraternity row were put here. Fraternities and sororities built their houses in accord with a policy, established by the University in 1959, that limited residents to six per house, limited construction costs, and gave title to Vanderbilt in return for advancing two-thirds of the money.

Sigma Alpha Epsilon alone opted for keeping an old house, this one on the corner of Kensington Place and Twenty-fifth, built in 1910 by Robert W. Turner as a private home.

By 1978 twenty-one new chapter houses were built in "fraternity row."
This is Sigma Chi, on Vanderbilt Place at Twenty-fifth, with Chi Omega next.

On the north side of Kensington Place,
Sigma Nu and Pi Kappa Alpha, with
Carmichael Towers standing tall beyond.

On south side of Kensington Place,
Alpha Omicron Pi (nearest camera)
and Gamma Phi Beta next door.

On Twenty-fourth Avenue, Kappa Alpha Theta
and Phi Kappa Sigma. At lower right is
Beta Theta Pi, on the northeast corner of
Vanderbilt Place and Twenty-fourth.

Branscomb Quadrangle, with rooms for 700, housed only women when opened in 1962. Lupton House, here, is largest of the four dormitories.

Inside the curved bay windows is Branscomb's formal parlor.

Parquet floor and panelled walls lend warmth to the music room.

This shows the South Dining Room when quadrangle was new.

Common rooms include lounges at the end of each dormitory floor.

The Tenth Decade

Formal installation of Alexander Heard as Chancellor of the University by Board President Harold Vanderbilt was on Library Lawn October 4, 1963.

At left of President Kennedy are Chancellor Heard and Governor Frank Clement. Congressman Richard Fulton is seated at right.

President John F. Kennedy came to Vanderbilt on a sunny Saturday morning, May 18, 1963, and spoke in commemoration of the founding of the University ninety years earlier. A bronze plaque at the Stadium commemorates his appearance and quotes his words:"The essence of Vanderbilt is still learning. The essence of its outlook is still liberty . . . Liberty without learning is always in peril, and learning without liberty is always in vain."

Commemorative plaque was placed on the concrete wall of Section A. It was the first anniversary of his visit and six months after his death. The principals in the ceremony were Chancellor Heard (on the left), Michael Ainslie as President of the Student Association, and Professor Robert T. Lagemann representing the faculty.

Stevenson Center

Stevenson Center for the Natural Sciences was constructed in three major phases from 1963 to 1974. More than any earlier Vanderbilt structure, it consciously created attractive open spaces between its buildings, all seven of which are connected underground. It houses the departments of Mathematics, Physics & Astronomy, Chemistry, Molecular Biology, Geology, and also the Science Library and the Computer Center. The view above is from the General Library.

Opposite page, clockwise from top left:
Computer Center, round as a biscuit.
  Lower courtyard, spiral staircase, and windows of Science Library seen from beneath Molecular Biology building.
  Upper courtyard, with low Lecture Hall on left, tall Chemistry building on right.
  One of four lighted Lucite panels by sculptor Nancy duPont Reynolds at entrance to the Sarah Stevenson Science Library.

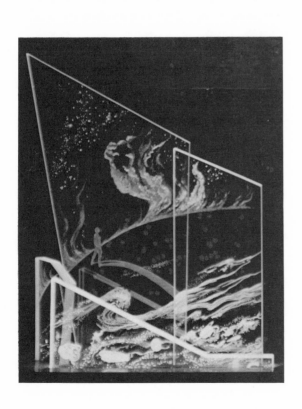

Carmichael Towers were built
two at a time, 1966 and 1970,
on West End at Twenty-fourth.
They house 1,200 students, many
in apartment-type quarters.
One of the lounges in the
Towers is pictured above.

Oldest and newest dormitories,
a West Side Row cottage and
the 14-story Carmichael Towers,
were contrasted in this picture
that was on the cover of the
1970 campus telephone book.
The photo below was made
in the "Different Drummer," a
Carmichael recreation room.

The University Club of Nashville, on Garland at Twenty-fourth, opened in 1969 and expanded the former Vanderbilt Faculty Club to include other institutions.

Alexander Hall was originally a funeral home built in 1954 on West End facing Centennial Park, from where this photograph was made. It was given to the University in 1969 and converted to quarters for the Owen Graduate School of Management.

McGugin Center was built in 1969
primarily for varsity athletes
and Athletic Department offices.
It is on Jess Neely Drive
facing the Stadium.

On Twenty-fifth Avenue opposite
Lewis and Morgan houses, the
Indoor Tennis Center covers four courts.
It was erected in 1977.

The Centennial Years

For contrast, compare the photograph below with the woodcut on page 43 and the photograph on page 44. The University itself is now like a city, an urban complex within a metropolitan area of more than half a million population. The aerial view below looks to the southwest. The street is Twenty-first Avenue. Facing it are, left to right, the Medical Center, the School of Nursing, and the Library, with Stevenson Center in the middle ground and the white Veterans Administration Hospital and Olin Hall of Engineering this side of the high-rise Lewis and Morgan apartments.

Vanderbilt celebrated its centennial with special focus on three anniversaries: March 17, 1973, centennial of the founding gift from the Commodore; April 28, 1974, centennial of the laying of the cornerstone of the Main Build-

ing; and October 3, 1975, centennial of the opening for classes. At the last of these ceremonies, members of the Vanderbilt faculty made the academic procession resplendent by wearing the robes and regalia of 177 universities that had conferred their highest degrees.

For help in solving problems of the 1970s, Vanderbilt turned to Richard Dober, of Cambridge, who had counseled Harvard and M.I.T. His objective was more specialized than previous plans; his 1970 study *(opposite page)* determined the site of Sarratt Student Center and showed how the old campus could be linked coherently with areas added south and southwest, and proposed doing it with broadwalks—pedestrian paths as wide as streets.

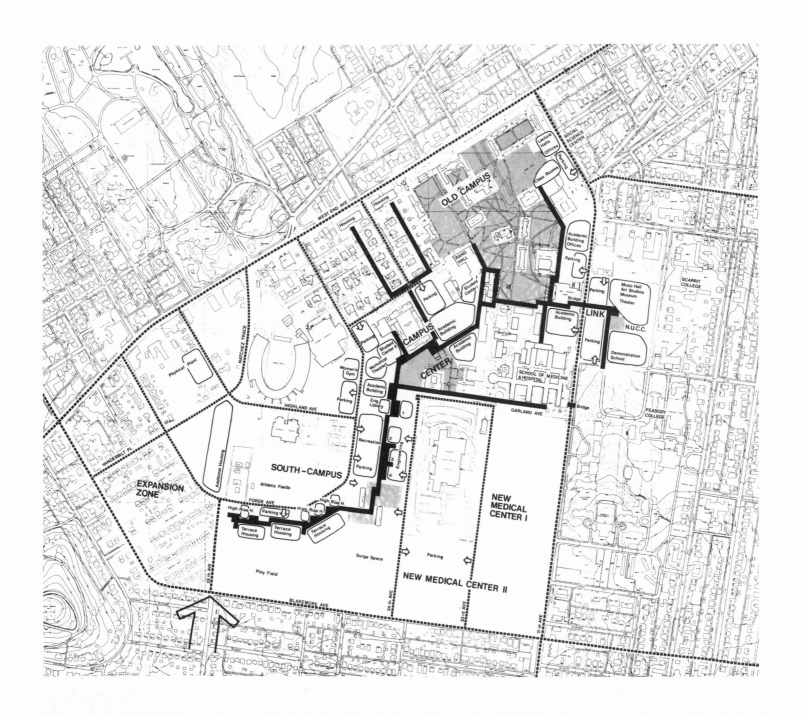

113

West End Avenue is at bottom of this 1974 photo, then Old Gym and Alumni Lawn. Vehicles on lawn belonged to Sarratt's construction crew.

Sarratt Student Center at twilight.

Madison Sarratt, friend of students
and alumni, 1916 to death in 1978.

West steps of Sarratt Student Center.

Main lobby of Sarratt Student Center. Exit left is toward Vanderbilt Place. Glass doors on right open to the sculpture courtyard.

Sarratt Student Center was the first Vanderbilt building
whose construction budget included a designated portion
(2% in its case) for art integral to the building.
Lawrence Anthony's humorous copper sculpture at right
caricatures eighteen "campus types."

Lounge in Sarratt, viewed from an interior balcony.
Architects for the building were Street & Street.

The facility houses radio station WRVU and student publications.

OF ENGINEERING

Olin Hall of Engineering
was completed in 1975
on Garland Avenue at
Twenty-fourth. It houses
Chemical Engineering
and Materials Science.

Chaffin Place, built in 1974
next to high-risers Lewis and
Morgan, is a group of six
buildings containing 48 flats
and apartments for 192 students.
This view is from the
Twenty-fourth Avenue side.

Mayfield Place opened in 1977, just south of Lewis
and Morgan. It is a group of 20 two-story apartments,
each accommodating ten students in single rooms.

On March 17, 1973, the hundredth anniversary of Cornelius Vanderbilt's founding gift, the University entertained his descendants for a family reunion. Counting spouses and children, 124 came. Trustee William H. Vanderbilt, in cap and gown, is near center of front row.

Magnolia wreath then placed at Harold Vanderbilt's statue
by Chancellor Emeritus Harvie Branscomb, on right, and the
Commodore's great-great-great grandson, John George
Vanderbilt Henry Spencer-Churchill, Duke of Marlborough.

Growth of Vanderbilt Medical Center

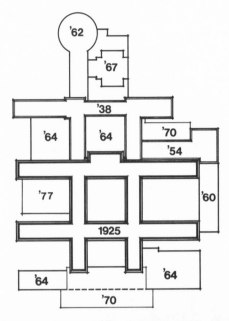

Vanderbilt Medical Center opened in September 1925 with 208 patient beds. Over the years it expanded in all directions and several architectural styles to become the complex structure that dominates the foreground of the aerial photograph at right, taken from a helicopter in April 1974, when the Medical Center occupied a 10-acre corner of the original campus. Here in the 1970s were more than 750,000 square feet of floor space, 501 beds and 45 bassinets, and facilities for teaching, research, and training. Faculty, staff, students, patients, visitors together made the daily population about 6,000.

The photograph below shows the original building under construction. The diagram at left dates the additions.

Above: The original entrance
to the School of Medicine was
through the carved stone doorway
near the center of the photo.

Right: The A.B. Learned Laboratory
was added onto the two wings,
two of the stories shown here
in 1952, seven more in 1961.

Left: The original entrance to Vanderbilt University Hospital was this carved stone archway facing Twenty-first Avenue.

Below: The old facade gave way to the Joe and Howard Werthan Building, which was added to the front of the Hospital in 1972.

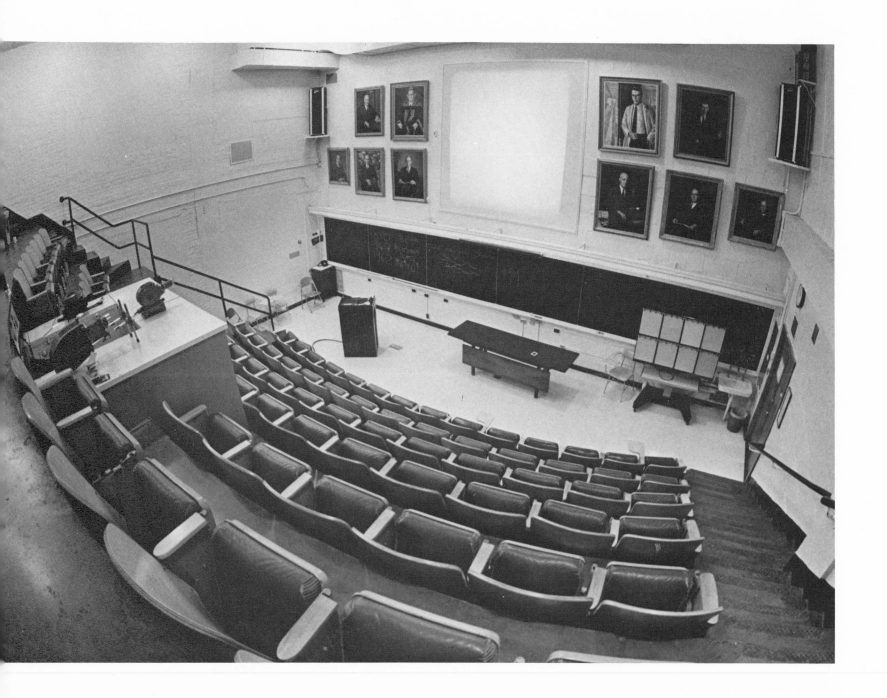

Zerfoss Student Health Center, itself a small hospital adjacent to Vanderbilt Hospital, opened in 1967. It is on the site of the residence that was built for Bishop McTyeire.

Left:
Amphitheater in the Medical Center.

Right:
West Wing of the Hospital, more often called "Round Wing," was built in 1962. Patients' rooms surround the nurses' station on each floor, increasing visibility and diminishing distances.

The significance of this picture is that the concrete slab
in the middle is the roof, not long before it was covered
with two feet of earth, of Vanderbilt's first underground
building. Put into use by the School of Nursing in the fall
of 1978, it contains three large lecture halls and several
smaller classrooms, and occupies underground space between
the school's main building *(on right of photograph)* and the
Stevenson Center for the Natural Sciences *(walls at left)*.

School of Nursing exterior is almost unchanged
since 1925 and this early photograph of it,
but interior has been entirely remodeled. In 1971
the building was renamed Godchaux Hall.

This 1974 aerial view from above Peabody campus looks across Twenty-first Avenue to Vanderbilt's expansion space. Street along the righthand edge is Garland Avenue. The Medical Arts Building is left of Garland at Twenty-first. The Medical Center is just out of sight to the right.

Looking down a new street, Twenty-second Avenue, in August 1978, with the new 514-bed Hospital under construction on the left, the new, 1,400-car parking garage on the right, and the old Hospital at the end of the new street.

The architectural rendering in perspective at left depicts the new Hospital completed, as it is scheduled to be in 1980. At lower left is the rounded corner of the 1,400-car parking garage. Beyond the Hospital is Rudolph A. Light Hall for medical education, completed in 1977, and the octagonal Langford Auditorium, completed in 1978. The photograph above, made from about the same viewpoint, shows the actual scene in September 1978.

Opposite page: Four pictures taken in Rudolph A. Light Hall, which was put into service in 1977. Clockwise from upper left, the scenes are one of the large rooms for lectures, the front lobby, the open gallery on the west side of the building, and the lounge.

Light Hall was not only needed in order to make medical education more efficient, it was required in order to accommodate a doubling of enrollment. The School of Medicine admitted approximately 50 new students a year from 1925 through 1966, then increased gradually until the number reached 103 in 1977.

Interior of Langford Auditorium is shown here in two views, looking toward the stage during a performance and looking from the stage. Although attached to Light Hall, a Medical School facility, Langford was designed to serve the entire University. It seats 1,200 and was first used in September 1978.

Engineering Dean Olin Landreth and his wife were photographed in rocking chairs on their back porch, probably in the 1880s. The house, oldest one on campus, is Old Central, still there, and the big tree beyond, a bur oak, grows beside it yet.

At left: This brick walk, pictured in the early 1920s, was Chancellor Kirkland's usual path from office toward home, straight ahead through the trees. This area became the site of the Stevenson Center.

The Trees

The tree beyond the porch in the picture at left is one of a pair of bur oaks near Old Central. The other, pictured on page 15, is the larger of the two, fourteen feet around at breast height. They are older than the University by far. Almost all other trees that shade the campus now were planted since the founding, many of them at the outset by Bishop McTyeire himself or at his direction. He planted so many that in time some had to be cleared out. His biographer wrote, "A friend asked one day, 'Don't you hate to see those fine young trees go down?' 'I don't see it, sir,' the Bishop replied. 'I can't stand it. I have to turn my back.'"

Chancellor Kirkland's biographer wrote that Kirkland was so regretful of the destruction of trees when new buildings had to take their places that "he would leave town to avoid the sight."

Chancellor Branscomb was assured in advance of Kissam Quadrangle's construction that two magnificent bald cypress trees growing there would be preserved. However, they were not. After retiring in 1963 and reflecting on things done or undone that he yet might do something about, he wrote a check that paid for planting six cypress trees. His wife Margaret is represented by magnolias growing in long rows at the edges of the campus along West End and Twenty-first avenues. The evergreen screen was her idea.

Chancellor Heard, for more than a year after taking office, required that his personal permission be obtained before any tree, living or dead, could be cut down. When persuaded that an assistant could make these decisions, he delegated the authority but said, in writing, "I warn you sternly against authorizing the elimination of trees unnecessarily."

Students also care. An example occurred in 1969, when architects designed a complex of buildings to house the social sciences at the center of the campus, taking much of the ground between Neely Auditorium and Garland Hall. The plan would erase Old Central and Old Science Hall, but in the eyes of students its chief fault was the loss of grass and trees. They organized a committee called "Save Open Space" — SOS — that bought full-page ads in the *Hustler* and called for reconsideration. A sophomore wrote an eloquent letter to Chancellor Heard on the importance of the natural areas of the campus to the satisfactions of life at Vanderbilt. The Chancellor ordered stakes placed to make clear how much land and which trees would be sacrificed. Too much and too many, he decided. The plans were shelved.

In 1879, six years after the founding, the University published a catalog of species and varieties of trees, shrubs, and woody vines "in the Vanderbilt Arboretum." A count of the species (minus varieties) of trees therein comes to 125 at least and possibly 140 depending on how one sees the vague line between trees and shrubs. The old catalog does not include conifers, which presumably waited on a sequel to be published that never was. The most numerous genus in 1879 were the oaks, seventeen different species. A century later, there were fifteen species of oaks growing on campus, and at least ten of these included individual oaks a hundred or more years old, veterans of the 1879 catalog.

Besides the oaks, species yet represented by trees that McTyeire planted a century ago, judged from their size in 1978, are the southern magnolia, the tulip-poplar, sugar maple, American and September elms, catalpa, beech, redbud, yellowwood, white ash, bald cypress, and perhaps a few others including two exotics from Asia, the massive ginkgo just north of Kirkland Hall and the pair of rare zelkova behind the Divinity School.

Aluminum labels, imprinted everlastingly with standard scientific and common names of trees, identify most of the largest specimens on campus and the trees alongside the most traveled walks. On last count there were more than 700 trees of 86 different species so marked.

After James Mapheus Smith, Ph.D. '31, died in 1968, his widow, who was librarian at Vanderbilt when he was a graduate student, endowed a memorial fund for labeling trees on the campus they both loved. The nails are stainless steel, not to hurt the tree. The springs between labels and nailheads allow several years' growth before adjustment is needed.

The Garland Oak leans outward from the left
of this picture, taken in the early 1900s.
David Douglas, holding the reins of the
horse-drawn rake, was superintendent of grounds
for the first thirty years. Virgil Henley,
his helper standing at right, served
the campus forty years.

On March 17, 1973, hundredth anniversary
of the founding, students representing
each of the schools took turns in planting
a young oak near the Garland Oak's old site.
Marsha Vande Berg wields shovel here.

Big trees older than Vanderbilt shade Stevenson Center's upper courtyard.

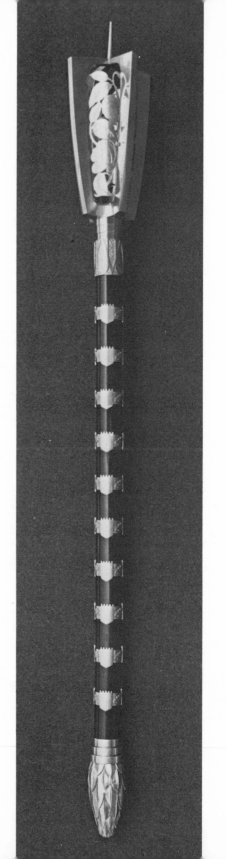

The gateway at the main entrance on West End Avenue displays its gilded V's against a background screen of evergreen magnolia trees.

Left:
Vanderbilt's ceremonial mace of rosewood and
vermeil is banded with engraved oak leaves
alternating with shields. Between the blades,
magnolias alternate with irises, and the
knock is in the form of a magnolia seedcone.

Commencement. A happy graduate, her new bachelor's degree certified by diploma in hand, is congratulated by Chancellor Heard as her name is announced by Dean Jacque Voegeli at the microphone during the 1976 Commencement ceremonies. A sycamore spreads leafy branches above its characteristic mottled trunk. Magnolia leaves decorate the front of the stage. Seven thousand chairs are placed on Curry Field, site of the event since 1971.

Commencement scene, May 11, 1977: Banners emblazoned with Vanderbilt's shield (embattled, charged with oak leaf and acorn). Trees. Tower. Sky.

In Memory of —

ALEXANDER, Henry Clay, 1902-1969. Vanderbilt '23. President of J. P. Morgan Company and later Chairman of Morgan Guarantee Trust Company, New York. Member of the Board of Trust 1947-1969; Vice-President of the Board 1955-1969. Alexander Hall, Owen Graduate School of Management.

ALUMNI. Alumni Memorial Hall is a memorial to the 44 Vanderbilt alumni who died in World War I. Memorial Gymnasium is a memorial to all Vanderbilt men and women who served in the armed forces in World War II.

ANDERSON, William Joseph, 1882-1963. Vanderbilt '05. Track coach, 1906 through 1948. Anderson Field.

BARNARD, Edward Emerson, 1857-1923. Vanderbilt '87. Reared in poverty and without formal schooling, he began work at age nine in a Nashville photographer's studio to support his invalid mother and himself—and became one of the world's most eminent astronomers. Four years at Vanderbilt as a special student and instructor in practical astronomy, 1883-1887, led to appointments at Lick Observatory, where he discovered the fifth satellite of Jupiter, and at Yerkes Observatory. He was the first to photograph the star clouds of the Milky Way and was recognized as the highest authority on comets and the Milky Way. Barnard Hall, dormitory.

BENTON, John Keith, 1896-1956. Dean of the Divinity School and Professor of Psychology and Philosophy of Religion, 1939-1956. Benton Chapel.

BRANSCOMB, Harvie and Margaret, 1894— and 1896—. Vanderbilt's fourth Chancellor, 1946-1963, and his wife. Branscomb Quadrangle, dormitory complex.

BRYAN, Edward Everett, 1901—. Vanderbilt '23. Superintendent of Buildings and Grounds for most of the years, 1924-1971, of his employment. Bryan Building, plant operations offices.

BUTTRICK, Wallace, 1853-1926. From 1902 to 1926 an officer of the General Education Board, an agency of Rockefeller philanthropy that gave Vanderbilt massive support in the 1920s for the School of Medicine and the College of Arts and Science. Buttrick Hall.

CALHOUN, William Henry, a Nashville jeweler, died shortly after the Civil War. A bequest from his daughter, Mary Ella Calhoun Foote, who died in 1918, provided half the funds to build Calhoun Hall.

CARMICHAEL, Oliver Cromwell, 1891-1966. Vanderbilt's third Chancellor, 1937-1946. Carmichael Towers, dormitories.

CARNEGIE, Andrew, 1835-1919. Scottish-born American industrialist and philanthropist. Part of the 1925 Medical School was designated as the Carnegie Building.

CHAFFIN, Nora Campbell, 1900—. Dean of Women and Professor of History, 1944-1966. Chaffin Place, student apartments.

COLE, Whitefoord Russell, 1874-1934. Vanderbilt '94. President of the NC&StL and L&N railroads. Member of the Board of Trust 1899-1934; President of the Board 1915-1934. Cole Hall, dormitory.

CURREY, Brownlee Owen, 1900-1952. Vanderbilt '23. Nashville investment banker. Member of the Board of Trust, 1947-1952. Currey Hall, dormitory in Kissam Quadrangle.

CURRY, Irby Rice, 1894-1918. Vanderbilt '16. Student leader and athlete, varsity quarterback four years, team captain 1916. World War I pilot, killed in air over France. Curry Field.

DUDLEY, William Lofland, 1859-1914. Professor of Chemistry 1886-1914; Dean of School of Medicine 1895-1913. Organized Southern Intercollegiate Athletic Association, first association of its kind, in 1893 and was its president to 1913. Name was given to Vanderbilt's old athletic field, renamed Curry Field in 1922 when Dudley's name was transferred to the field in the Stadium.

DYER, Arthur J., 1868-1957. Vanderbilt '91. Founder and President of Nashville Bridge Company. Principal patron of Dyer Observatory.

FLOWERS, Henry Fort, 1888-1975. Vanderbilt '12. Inventor and industrialist, Findlay, Ohio. H. Fort Flowers Graduate Wing of the General Library.

FURMAN, Francis, 1816-1899. Nashville wholesale drygoods merchant. His widow's bequest provided for building of Furman Hall.

GALLOWAY, Charles Betts, 1849-1909. Methodist Bishop, member of Vanderbilt Board of Trust 1894-1909; President of the Board 1905-1909. Galloway Memorial Hospital on South Campus was named for him, and name was transferred in 1925 to a major portion of the new Hospital.

GARLAND, Landon Cabell, 1810-1895. Vanderbilt's first Chancellor, 1875-1893, and Professor of Physics and Astronomy to 1895. Garland Hall.

GODCHAUX, Mary Ragland (Mrs. Frank A. Godchaux, Jr.), 1902-1970. Member of family prominent in Vanderbilt affairs for four generations. Godchaux Hall, School of Nursing.

HEMINGWAY, Wilson Linn, 1880-1954. Vanderbilt '00. Little Rock and St. Louis banker, President of American Bankers Association 1942. Member of the Board of Trust 1917-1954; President of the Board 1950-1954. Hemingway Hall, dormitory in Kissam Quadrangle.

KIRKLAND, James Hampton and Mary Henderson, 1859-1939 and 1867-1950. Vanderbilt's second Chancellor, 1893-1937, and his wife. Kirkland Hall, main administration building.

KISSAM, Maria Louisa (Mrs. William Henry Vanderbilt), 1821-1896. Mother of William Kissam Vanderbilt, the Commodore's grandson who gave the original Kissam Hall in her memory. Name transferred to Kissam Quadrangle.

LANGFORD, Lilburn C., 1893-1977. Nashville business man, developer of chain of 129 restaurants. His widow donated a major portion of the funds for Langford Auditorium.

LEARNED, Andrew Brown, 1869-1961. Vanderbilt '89. Natchez lumber man. Donor of major funds for Learned Laboratory.

LEWIS, Fred Justin, 1890-1959. Dean of the School of Engineering, 1933-1959. Lewis House, student apartments.

LIGHT, Rudolph Alvin, 1909-1970. Vanderbilt M.D. '39. Member of School of Medicine faculty 1948-1958; member of the Board of Trust 1964-1970. Major donor to Vanderbilt in his lifetime and through his will. Light Hall, School of Medicine.

LIGHT, S. Rudolph, 1877-1961. Physician of Kalamazoo, Michigan, and executive of Upjohn pharmaceutical company. S. Rudolph Light Laboratory for Surgical Research.

LITTERER, William, 1832-1917. Business man, once Mayor of Nashville, donor in 1915 of the building at 631 Second Avenue, South, that formerly was owned by the University of Nashville. In 1925 the name was perpetuated in the microbiology laboratories of the new School of Medicine.

LUPTON, Kate (Mrs. L. W. Wilkinson), 1859-1897. First woman to receive a Vanderbilt degree, Master of Arts in 1879. She was the daughter of the University's first professor of chemistry, Nathanael T. Lupton, and she herself became a college teacher. Lupton House, dormitory in Branscomb Quadrangle.

MAYFIELD, George Radford, 1877-1964. Vanderbilt M.A. '04, Ph.D. '15. He came to Vanderbilt in 1903 as a graduate student and was a member of the faculty 43 years, retiring in 1947 as Professor of German. Prominent conservationist, he was a founder of the Tennessee Ornithological Society. Mayfield Place, student apartments.

McGILL, John Thomas, 1851-1946. Vanderbilt '79, Ph.D. '81. A founder of the Alumni Association, its second President 1881-82, and connected with Vanderbilt 70 years, from 1876 when he matriculated as a student until 1946 when he died at his home on campus. He retired in 1920 as Professor of Organic Chemistry and Dean of the School of Pharmacy, but continued until 1942 as Secretary of Phi Beta Kappa and until 1946 as Historian of the Alumni Association. McGill Hall, dormitory, faces the former site of the McGill residence.

McGUGIN, Daniel Earl, 1879-1936. Head football coach, 1904 through 1934 season. McGugin Center and McGugin Field.

McTYEIRE, Holland Nimmons, 1824-1889. Methodist Bishop, chief organizer of the University, the man to whom Cornelius Vanderbilt made his founding gift, and President of the Board of Trust from 1873 until he died. McTyeire Hall, dormitory.

MIMS, Edwin, 1872-1959. Vanderbilt '92. Professor of English and Chairman of the English Department from 1912 until he retired in 1942. Author of *Chancellor Kirkland of Vanderbilt* and *History of Vanderbilt University*. Mims Hall, dormitory in Kissam Quadrangle.

MORGAN, Hugh Jackson, 1893-1961. Vanderbilt '14. Member of the faculty 1925-1958, Professor of Medicine and Head of the Department of Medicine 1935-1958, Chief Medical Consultant to the Surgeon General of the U. S. Army in World War II. Morgan House, student apartments.

NEELY, George Mitchell, died 1922. Member of the Board of Trust 1902-1922, and Treasurer of the University. His widow donated the funds to build Neely Auditorium.

OBERLIN, John Frederick, 1740-1826. Alsatian pastor whose life inspired the founders of Oberlin College. The Oberlin Graduate School of Theology merged with Vanderbilt Divinity School in 1966, and the Board of Trust in 1970 applied his name to the Divinity Quadrangle.

OLIN, Franklin W., 1860-1951. American industrialist. The Olin Foundation granted the funds to build Olin Hall of Engineering.

PARMER, Walter O., 1855-1932. Nashville Thoroughbred horse breeder, owner of Belle Meade Farm 1916-1932. Donor of funds to build Parmer Club House at Dudley Field in 1922.

RAND, Frank Chambless, 1876-1949. Vanderbilt '98. President and Chairman of International Shoe Company, St. Louis. Member of the Board of Trust 1912-1949; President of the Alumni Association 1918-1920; President of the Board of Trust 1935-1949. Rand Hall.

REINKE, Edwin Eustace, 1887-1945. Professor of Biology and Chairman of the Biology Department, 1915-1945. Reinke Hall, dormitory in Kissam Quadrangle.

SARRATT, Charles Madison, 1888-1978. "Professor of Mathematics, Head of the Department of Mathematics, Dean of Students, Chairman of Athletics, Vice-Chancellor, Acting Chancellor, Vice-Chancellor Emeritus and Dean of Alumni, Friend of Students and Alumni from 1916 to 1978" — so reads the memorial plaque in Sarratt Student Center.

SCALES, Ann (Mrs. Andrew Bell Benedict), 1883-1958. Vanderbilt '05. Leader of alumnae, especially in the movement that gave the University its first Dean of Women in 1925. Scales House, dormitory in Branscomb Quadrangle.

STAPLETON, Ada Bell, died 1947. First woman member of the Vanderbilt faculty, 1925-1947, and Dean of Women 1925-1940. Stapleton House, dormitory in Branscomb Quadrangle.

STEVENSON, Eldon B., Jr., 1893-1972. Vanderbilt '14. President of National Life and Accident Insurance Company, Nashville. President of the Alumni Association 1934-1938; member of the Board of Trust 1938-1972; chairman of the $30 million campaign 1960-1962; principal individual contributor of funds that built Stevenson Center for the Natural Sciences.

TOLMAN, Herbert Cushing, 1865-1923. Professor of Greek 1894-1923; founder of Vanderbilt chapter of Phi Beta Kappa 1901; Dean of the College of Arts and Science 1914-1923. Tolman Hall, dormitory.

UNDERWOOD, Peter Fondren, 1933-1951. Died at age 17 in an automobile accident near his home in Houston, Texas. His father, Milton R. Underwood, Vanderbilt '28 and member of the Board of Trust, donated funds for Underwood Auditorium in his memory.

VANDERBILT, Frederick William, 1856-1938. Grandson of the Commodore, he left a large part of his estate to the University. Frederick Vanderbilt Hall, dormitory.

VAUGHN, Stella Scott, 1871-1960. Vanderbilt '96. She grew up on the campus, daughter of the head of the Mathematics Department, William J. Vaughn. She originated Vanderbilt's first physical education program for women and was unofficial dean of women before that position became official in 1925. Vaughn House, dormitory in Branscomb Quadrangle.

WERTHAN, Joe and Howard, 1889-1967 and 1914-1967. Father and son, executives of Werthan Bag Company, Nashville. The Werthan family has provided support for several Vanderbilt endeavors, mainly in the medical fields. Werthan Building.

WESLEY, John, 1703-1791. Anglican clergyman, founder of Methodism. Wesley Hall.

WILLS, William Ridley, 1871-1949. A founder and later President of National Life and Accident Insurance Company, Nashville. Member of the Board of Trust 1935-1938. His widow and children established the W. R. Wills Center for Psychiatric Treatment and Research.

ZERFOSS, Thomas Bowman and Kate Savage, 1895— and 1895—. Vanderbilt '17 and '18, respectively, and both Doctors of Medicine, he Vanderbilt '22, she Tulane '22. He served students from 1926 to 1962 as University Physician. Zerfoss Student Health Center.

Architects

1853-54. University of Nashville building on South Campus. Adolphus Heiman.

1859(?). Old Central. Architect not known.

1875. Main Building. Observatory, and eight homes for faculty. William C. Smith. 1906 remodeling of Main Building by Carpenter & Blair, New York.

1880. Wesley Hall. Peter J. Williamson. (Destroyed by fire, 1932.)

1880. Science Hall. Peter J. Williamson.

1880. Gymnasium. Peter J. Williamson. 1962 remodeling of interior by F. B. Warfield & Associates.

1880s. Admissions Office. Architect not known.

1886-87. West Side Row. Olin H. Landreth.

1887. West Side Hall. Olin H. Landreth.

1888. Mechanical Engineering Hall. William C. Smith.

1889. Dental and Law building on Fourth Avenue. T. Leach Dismukes. (Razed in 1970.)

1895. Medical School building at Fifth and Elm. Julian C. Zwicker. (Razed in 1930s.)

1900(?). Litterer Laboratory on Second Avenue. Brown & Brown (?).

1901. Kissam Hall. Hunt & Hunt, New York. (Razed in 1958.)

1902. Master plan for campus. Hunt & Hunt, New York.

1905. Master plan for campus. George E. Kessler, Kansas City.

1907. Furman Hall. Snelling & Potter, New York. 1967 remodeling by Street & Street.

1910. Sigma Alpha Epsilon fraternity. Architect not known.

1922. Stadium. Hart & Nevins.

1924. Master plan for campus. Day & Klauder, Philadelphia.

1925. Alumni Memorial Hall. Henry C. Hibbs.

1925. Neely Auditorium. Henry C. Hibbs. 1976 remodeling of interior by Peter Blake and Brian Smith, New York, with David Hays, consultant.

1925. Medical Center. Coolidge & Shattuck, Boston, 1938 addition by Henry C. Hibbs. 1955-1972 additions by John A. Preston.

1925. Godchaux Hall. Coolidge & Shattuck, Boston. 1978 addition by Earl Swensson.

1925. Power Plant. Coolidge & Shattuck, Boston. 1965 addition Reese & Jackson.

1927. Wesley Hall (former Y.M.C.A. Graduate School). Henry C. Hibbs.

1928. Buttrick, Calhoun, and Garland halls. Henry C. Hibbs.

1934. Bryan Building (Plant Operations). Asmus & Clark.

1940. McTyeire Hall. Warfield & Keeble.

1941. Joint University Libraries main building. Henry C. Hibbs. 1969 addition by Shepley, Bulfinch, Richardson & Abbott, Boston.

1947. McGill and Tolman halls. F. B. Warfield & Associates.

1947. Master plan for campus. Edward Durell Stone, New York.

1948. Theater. F. B. Warfield & Associates. (Razed in 1975.)

1949. Cole Hall, F. B. Warfield & Associates.

1950. School of Engineering. Hart, Freeland & Roberts.

1951. Medical Arts Building. Marr & Holman.

1952. Barnard and Frederick Vanderbilt halls. F. B. Warfield & Associates.

1952. Memorial Gymnasium. Edwin A. Keeble.

1952. Purchasing Department building (former Athletic Department offices). Brush, Hutchison & Gwinn.

1953. Learned Laboratories. Donald Southgate. 1961 addition by John A. Preston.

1953. Dyer Observatory. Clarence and Bruce Jones, Chattanooga.

1953. Rand Hall. F. B. Warfield & Associates, with Edward Durell Stone, New York, consultant.

1954. Alexander Hall. Wallace & Clemmons.

1957. Kissam Quadrangle. Edward Durell Stone, New York.

1959. Divinity School. Brush, Hutchison & Gwinn.

1960. Entrance gate, West End Avenue. William Platt, New York.

1960. Kappa Sigma fraternity. Burkhalter & Hickerson.

1961. Sigma Chi fraternity. Taylor & Crabtree.

1962. School of Law. Brush, Hutchison & Gwinn.

1962. Alpha Epsilon Pi fraternity. Woolwine, Harwood & Clark.

1962. Alpha Omicron Pi sorority. Street & Street.

1962. Delta Delta Delta sorority. Terrill Hall.

1962. Kappa Alpha Theta sorority. Brush, Hutchison & Gwinn.

1962. Pi Kappa Alpha fraternity. Taylor & Crabtree.

1962. Branscomb Quadrangle. Brush, Hutchison & Gwinn.

1962. Lewis and Morgan houses. Brush, Hutchison & Gwinn.

1962. Oxford House. W. G. McComas.

1963. Stevenson Center for the Natural Sciences. Shepley, Bulfinch, Richardson & Abbott, Boston.

1963. Beta Theta Pi fraternity. Hart, Freeland & Roberts.

1963. Delta Kappa Epsilon fraternity. Rodgers & Rodgers.

1963. Gamma Phi Beta sorority. Warterfield & Bass.

1963. Phi Delta Theta fraternity. Edwin A. Keeble.

1963. Sigma Nu fraternity. Reese & Jackson.

1964. Alpha Tau Omega fraternity. McComas & Moneypenny.

1964. Chi Omega sorority. Rodgers & Rodgers.

1964. Kappa Alpha fraternity. Brush, Hutchison & Gwinn.

1964. Kappa Delta sorority. Warterfield & Bass.

1964. Phi Kappa Sigma fraternity. Street & Street.

1964. Pi Beta Phi sorority. Taylor & Crabtree.

1964. Zeta Beta Tau fraternity. John Charles Wheeler.

1965. Master plan for campus. Clarke & Rapuano, New York.

1965. Phi Kappa Psi fraternity. Donald E. Stoll.

1966. Carmichael Towers. Brush, Hutchison & Gwinn

1967. Zerfoss Student Health Center. Street & Street.

1967. Medical Center South, Ost, Follis & Wagner, Memphis.

1969. McGugin Center. Yearwood & Johnson.

1969. University Club of Nashville. Brush, Hutchison & Gwinn.

1970. Master plan for campus. Dober, Paddock, Upton & Associates, Cambridge.

1974. Olin Hall of Engineering. Robinson Neil Bass.

1974. Sarratt Student Center. Street & Street.

1974. Chaffin Place. Gassner-Nathan-Browne, Memphis.

1977. Light Hall. Schmidt, Garden & Erikson, Chicago.

1977. Mayfield Place. Street & Street

1977. Parking Garage, Twenty-first and Garland. Arthur Cotton Moore, Washington.

1978. Kappa Kappa Gamma sorority. Street & Street.

1980. Hospital. Schmidt. Garden & Erikson, Chicago.

Picture Credits

Note: VUPA abbreviates Vanderbilt University Photographic Archive.

2. Hand-colored print, copyright 1977 by Southern Galleries, Hopkinsville, Ky., 42240. Used by permission of Harvey O. White.

5. J. Clark Thomas, 1976.

9. *Vanderbilt: Its Progress and Purposes,* 1926.

10. Left, map by Wilbur F. Foster, Major, Engineer Corps, C.S.A.
Right, Jane Word, 1978.

11. Map of Davidson County by Wilbur F. Foster, 1871, from Tennessee State Library and Archives.

12. Left, portrait by William J. Whittemore, 1906, photographed by Herb Peck, Jr., 1978.
Right, *Frank Leslie's Illustrated Newspaper,* New York, April 17, 1875.

13. Portrait by Jared Bradley Flagg, 1875, photographed by Herb Peck, Jr., 1978.

14. Tigert Collection, Vanderbilt University Archives, Joint University Libraries.

15. Ken Spain, 1956.

16. Harry S. Vaughn, Vaughn Collection, VUPA.

17. Diagram of parcels composing original campus based on manuscript map by John T. McGill, Vanderbilt University Archives.

18. Left, J. Clark Thomas, 1974. Right, courtesy Corinthian Lodge No. 414, F. & A.M.

19. Carl C. Giers, 1875, VUPA.

20. VUPA.

21. Left, 1888, John T. McGill Collection, VUPA.
Right, W.G. and A.J. Thuss, VUPA.

22. Map adapted from 1896 Vanderbilt catalog. Photograph VUPA.

23. Harry S. Vaughn, Vaughn Collection, VUPA.

24. Left, VUPA.
Right, J. Clark Thomas, 1973.

25. Left, Bill Humphrey in 1958 *Commodore*. p. 287.
Upper right, Ginger Carnahan for Office of Public Affairs, Vanderbilt Medical Center, 1978.
Lower right, VUPA.

26. Upper, Jane Word, 1978.
Lower, Dillard Jacobs, 1974.

27. Robert A. McGaw, 1978.

28. Left, VUPA.
Right, Italian Government Travel Office, New York.

29. Upper left, Carl C. Giers, 1875, VUPA.
Upper right, 1877, VUPA.
Lower left, ca. 1904, VUPA.
Lower right W. G. and A. J. Thuss, 1905 VUPA.

30. Left, Charles W. Warterfield, Jr., 1950.
Right, VUPA.

31. Upper left, 1909 *Commodore*, p. 415.
Middle, J. Clark Thomas, 1973.
Lower, Robert A. McGaw, 1978.

32. J. Clark Thomas, 1974.

33. Ken Spain, 1957.

34. VUPA.

35. Upper left, W. G. and A. J. Thuss, 1897, in *Art Album of the Tennessee Centennial,* Marshall & Bruce, 1898, VUPA.
Others by J. Clark Thomas, 1976.

36. Left, 1887 *Comet,* following page 56.
Right, Jack E. Boucher for Historic American Buildings Survey, 1970.

37. Drawn by William H. Edwards for Historic American Buildings Survey, 1970.

38. Jack E. Boucher for Historic American Buildings Survey, 1970.

39. Drawn by William H. Edwards for Historic American Buildings Survey, 1970.

40. Upper left, J. Clark Thomas, 1973.
Upper right, drawn by Donald W. Graham, Jr., and William H. Edwards for Historic American Buildings Survey, 1970.
Lower, VUPA.

41. Ken Spain in 1948 *Commodore*, p. 100.

42. Left, VUPA.
Right, John T. McGill collection, VUPA.

43. Woodcut by A. Little in W. W. Clayton's *History of Davidson County,* 1880.

44. Upper, VUPA.
Lower, 1923, VUPA.

45. Upper and lower right, Jack E. Boucher for Historic American Buildings Survey, 1971.
Lower left, J. Clark Thomas, 1974.

46. Upper left, portrait by Jared Bradley Flagg, 1877, photographed by Howard Cooper, 1973.
Upper right, J. Clark Thomas, 1974.
Lower, 1889 Vanderbilt catalog, p. 102.

47. Lloyd James Onstott in 1975 *Commodore,* p. 175.

48. 1888, John T. McGill Collection, VUPA.

49. Map by Granbery Jackson, 1897.

50. VUPA.

51. Upper, Harry S. Vaughn, Vaughn Collection, VUPA.
Lower, 1910 *Commodore,* p. 361.

52. Upper, 1892 *Comet,* p. 146.
Lower left, 1891, VUPA.
Lower right, late 1880s, gift of Elliston Farrell, VUPA.

53. 1892, John T. McGill Collection, VUPA.

54. Corbitt Photographers, VUPA.

55. Hunt & Hunt.

56. Upper, early 1950s, VUPA.
Lower, Marvin W. Wiles, 1910(?), VUPA.

57. Upper, VUPA.
Lower left, Hunt & Hunt
Lower right, VUPA.

58. 1898, VUPA.

59. VUPA.

60. Upper, VUPA.
Lower, VUPA.

·61. Drawn by H. Wright for George E. Kessler & Co., 1905.

62. Upper left, 1917 *Commodore,* p. 17.
Upper right, J. Clark Thomas, 1974.
Lower right, Harry S. Vaughn, Vaughn Collection, VUPA.

63. J. Clark Thomas, 1974.

64. Vanderbilt University Archives, Joint University Libraries.

65. Marvin W. Wiles, 1917 *Commodore* pp. 20-21. Map of Nashville, 1879, Nashville Board of Health.

66. Jack E. Boucher for Historic American Buildings Survey, 1970.

67. Upper, Marvin W. Wiles, VUPA.
Lower, Kay Beasley, 1978.

68. Left VUPA.
Right, 1888 Vanderbilt catalog, p. 78.

69. Map from 1913 Vanderbilt catalog.

70. VUPA.

71. Day & Klauder.

72. Upper, VUPA.

72-73. Vanderbilt Department of Athletics.

73. Upper left, Marvin W. Wiles, VUPA.
Upper right, 1927, VUPA.

74. Upper left, VUPA.
Upper right, Frank Gunter, *Vanderbilt Alumnus* cover, June, 1939.
Lower left, Barr-Hime Co., VUPA.
Lower right, J. Clark Thomas, 1976.

75. VUPA, Lower right, in 1945 *Commodore,* p. 176.

76. Walter M. Williams, VUPA.

77. Upper left, *Vanderbilt Alumnus,* February 1932, p. 97.
Upper right, VUPA.
Portrait by Paul Trebilcock, 1948, photographed by Howard Cooper, 1963.

78. J. Clark Thomas, 1974.

79. Upper, Howard Cooper, 1963.
Lower left, VUPA.
Lower right, J. Clark Thomas, 1974.

80. Upper, Jack Corn, 1961.
Lower left, VUPA.
Lower right, J. Clark Thomas, 1978.

81. Upper left, Jack Corn, 1961.
Upper right, Photographic Arts, Inc., in *Vanderbilt Alumnus,* April-May, 1947, p. 11.
Lower left, VUPA.
Lower right, in 1950 *Commodore,* p. 44, VUPA.

82. Edward Durell Stone.

83. Left, VUPA.
Portrait by Paul Trebilcock, 1959, photographed by Howard Cooper, 1963.

84. Upper, Ken Spain, 1952.
Lower, J. Clark Thomas, 1974.

85. Upper, Jack Howe, *Vanderbilt Alumnus* cover, January-February, 1953.
Lower, J. Clark Thomas.

86. Upper, *Vanderbilt Alumnus,* October-November, 1948, p. 10, VUPA.
Lower left, *The Nashville Tennessean,* 1949, VUPA.
Lower right, Ken Spain in 1958 *Commodore,* pp. 4-5.

87. Left, Bill Humphrey.
Right, William Thomas Edwards in 1975 *Commodore,* p. 360.

88. Upper, Ken Spain, 1954.
Lower, Robert A. McGaw, 1978.

89. Left, Ken Spain, 1950s.
Right, J. Clark Thomas, 1970s.

90. Charles W. Warterfield, Jr., 1950.

90-91. Map by A. F. Raymer, Edwin A. Keeble Associates, 1958.

92. Left, J. Clark Thomas, 1974.
Right, Howard Cooper, 1959-60.

93. Left, Dennis Wile, 1975/76.
Right, J. Clark Thomas, 1974.

94. Robert A. McGaw, 1978.

95. Howard Cooper, 1962.

96. C. David Philpo, 1976.

97. Left, Jane Word, 1978.
Right, Howard Cooper, 1962.

98. Clarke & Rapuano.

99. Robert A. McGaw, 1978.

100. Upper left and right, in 1928 *Commodore,* pp. 98-99, VUPA.
Middle and lower left, Robert A. McGaw, 1978.

101. Robert A. McGaw, 1978.

102. Howard Cooper, 1962.

103. Howard Cooper, 1962, except lower left, 1963.

104. Left, Leviton-Atlanta, 1963.
Right, Fred Travis, 1963.

105. Upper, Bill Goodman for *Nashville Banner,* 1964.
Lower, Jimmy Holt for *Nashville Tennessean,* 1963.

106. Upper, J. Clark Thomas, 1974.
Lower, John Lyda for Vanderbilt Campus Planning Office, 1974.

107. VUPA except upper right, J. Clark Thomas, 1973.

108. Left, J. Clark Thomas, 1974.
Right, J. Clark Thomas, 1973.

109. Left, J. Clark Thomas, 1973.
Right, Howard Cooper, 1970.

110. Upper, Dick Dempster, 1970.
Lower, Robert A. McGaw, 1978.

111. Upper, J. Clark Thomas, 1974.
Lower, John Lyda, 1978.

112. J. Clark Thomas, 1974.

113. Dober, Paddock, Upton & Associates.

114. J. Clark Thomas, 1974.

115. Upper left, J. Clark Thomas, 1974.
Lower left, J. Clark Thomas, 1973.
Right J. Clark Thomas, 1976.

116. J. Clark Thomas, 1974.

117. Left, J. Clark Thomas, 1974.
Upper right, John Lyda for Vanderbilt Campus Planning Office, 1976.
Lower right, J. Clark Thomas, 1978.

118. J. Clark Thomas, 1977.

119. Robert A. McGaw, 1978.

120. J. Clark Thomas, 1973.

121. J. Clark Thomas, 1973.

122. Diagram by John Lyda.
Lower, Williams & Nicks.

123. J. Clark Thomas, 1974.

124. Upper, VUPA.
Lower, Jack Corn, 1961.

125. Upper, VUPA.
Lower J. Clark Thomas, 1974.

126. J. Clark Thomas, 1977.

127. Upper, J. Clark Thomas, 1974.
Lower, Jack Corn, 1962.

128. John Lyda, 1978.

129. VUPA.

130. J. Clark Thomas, 1974.

131. Robert A. McGaw, 1978.

132-133. Schmidt, Garden & Erikson.

133. Robert A. McGaw, 1978.

134. Upper, Jane Word, 1978.
Lower, Robert A. McGaw, 1978.

135. Sadin/Karant Photography, Inc., for Schmidt, Garden & Erickson.

136. VUPA.

137. Courtesy of Mrs. Clifford (Mary E. Landreth) Parker.

138. J. Clark Thomas, 1978.

139. Left, J. Clark Thomas, 1973.
Right, Harry S. Vaughn, Vaughn Collection, VUPA.

140. VUPA.

141. Robert A. McGaw, 1978.

142. David Burnside in 1976 *Commodore,* p. 317.

143. Jane Word, 1977.

160. Robert A. McGaw, 1978.

Photographers

Barr-Hime Co., 74 lower left.

Kay Beasley, 67 lower.

Jack E. Boucher, 36 right, 38, 45 upper and lower right, 66.

David Burnside, 142.

Ginger Carnahan, 25 upper right

Howard Cooper, 46 upper left, 77 upper right, 79 upper, 83 right, 92 right, 95, 97 right, 102, 103, 109 right.

Corbitt Photographers, 54.

Jack Corn, 80 upper, 81 upper left, 124 lower, 127 lower.

Dick Dempster, 110 upper.

William Thomas Edwards, 87 right.

Carl C. Giers, 19, 29 upper left.

Bill Goodman, 105 upper.

Frank Gunter, 74 upper right.

Jimmy Holt, 105 lower.

Jack Howe, 85 upper.

Bill Humphrey, 25 left, 87 left.

Dillard Jacobs, 26 lower.

Leviton-Atlanta, 104 left.

John Lyda, 106 lower, 111 lower, 117 upper right, 128.

Robert A. McGaw, 27, 31 lower, 88 lower, 94, 99, 100 middle and lower left, 101, 110 lower, 119, 131, 133, 134 lower, 141, 160.

Lloyd James Onstott, 47.

Herb Peck, Jr., 12 left, 13.

C. David Philpo, 96.

Photographic Arts, Inc., 81 upper right.

Sadin/Karant Photography, Inc., 135

Ken Spain, 15, 33, 41, 84 upper, 86 lower right, 88 upper, 89 left.

J. Clark Thomas, 5, 18 left, 24 right, 31 middle, 32, 40 upper left, 45 lower left, 46 upper right, 62 upper right, 63, 74 lower right, 78, 79 lower right, 80 lower right, 84 lower, 85 lower, 89 right, 92 left, 93 right, 106 upper, 107 upper right, 108 left and right, 109 left, 111 upper, 112, 114, 115 upper left, lower left and right, 116, 117 left and lower right, 118, 120, 121, 123, 125 lower, 126, 127 upper, 130, 138, 139 left.

W. G. & A. J. Thuss, 21 right, 29 lower right, 35 upper left.

Fred Travis, 104 right.

Harry S. Vaughn, 16, 23, 51 upper, 62 lower right, 139 right.

Charles Warterfield, 30 left, 90.

Dennis Wile, 93.

Marvin W. Wiles, 56 lower, 65, 67 upper, 73 upper left.

Walter M. Williams, 76.

Williams & Nicks, 122 lower.

Jane Word, 10 right, 26 upper, 97 left, 134 upper, 143.

Index

Carved limestone panels set into the wall of the sculpture courtyard in
Sarratt Student Center depict the seals of the City of Nashville, on left,
and the State of Tennessee. The panels were salvaged from the facade of
Vanderbilt University Hospital when an addition was made to its front.

*Robert A. McGaw, who selected the pictures, designed the pages, and wrote
the essays and captions of this book, has lived near the campus since 1918. He
attended the College of Arts and Science, went into journalism, was employed
by Vanderbilt in 1948 as a staff assistant to the Chancellor, and was appointed
Secretary of the University in 1964. He has been a member of the Metropolitan
Nashville Historical Commission since it was established in 1966 and is chairman of the city's Historic Zoning Commission. He served as president of the
Tennessee Historical Society from 1969 to 1971, as chairman of the Tennessee
Historical Commission from 1969 to 1974, and is one of Tennessee's members
on the Advisory Board of the National Trust for Historic Preservation.*